Beyond the
<u>Cold War</u>

A closeup of the framed cartoon by a Russian artist presented by Soviet President Mikhail Gorbachev to U.S. President George Bush, September 1990. The cartoon depicts the two presidents as victorious boxers who have just knocked out the Cold War. Reprinted by permission of Reuters/Bettmann. Photo by Gary Cameron, Reuters.

Beyond the Cold War

Soviet and American Media Images

edited by

Everette E. Dennis
George Gerbner
Yassen N. Zassoursky

SAGE PUBLICATIONS
The International Professional Publishers
Newbury Park   London   New Delhi

For information address:

SAGE Publications, Inc.
2455 Teller Road
Newbury Park, California 91320

SAGE Publications Ltd.
6 Bonhill Street
London EC2A 4PU
United Kingdom

SAGE Publications India Pvt. Ltd.
M-32 Market
Greater Kailash I
New Delhi 110 048 India

Printed in the United States of America

Library of Congress Cataloging-in-Publication Data

Beyond the Cold War: Soviet and American media images / edited by
    Everette E. Dennis, George Gerbner, and Yassen N. Zassoursky.
        p.   cm.
    Papers from a bilateral conference held at Moscow State University
in June and July of 1989.
    Includes bibliographical references and index.
    ISBN 0-8039-3900-0. — ISBN 0-8039-3901-9 (pbk.)
    1. Soviet Union—Foreign public opinion, American.   2. United
States—Foreign public opinion, Soviet.   3. Soviet Union—Foreign
public opinion, Chinese.   4. United States—Foreign public opinion,
Chinese.   5. Public opinion—Soviet Union.   6. Public opinion—
United States.   7. Public opinion—China.   8. Mass media—Political
aspects—Soviet Union.   9. Mass media—Political aspects—United
States.   10. Mass media—Political aspects—China.   I. Dennis,
Everette E.   II. Gerbner, George.   III. Zassoursky, Yassen N.
E183.8.S65B5   1991
303.48'247073—dc20   90-23413
                                                                    CIP

FIRST PRINTING, 1991

Sage Production Editor: Michelle R. Starika

Contents

Preface

Any consideration of relationships between and among peoples necessarily must turn to the mass media, for it is in these instruments of communication that images are created and information is transmitted. Public diplomacy is played out in the public arena typically on television, in magazines, newspapers, books, and other media. Whereas there may be some information confined exclusively to the diplomatic pouch accessible only to governments and foreign policymakers, most of what we know about other countries comes from public media.

The images that emerge in public communication are not confined to a single media function, but instead embrace communication and news as well as opinion and entertainment. Although our first thoughts of media images might go to serious international news, such as that on television network programs or in newspapers and newsmagazines, images also are generated by opinion media—on editorial pages and in thought magazines. They are also found in entertainment media like television drama and situation comedies. Images contained in advertising and marketing, too, add to cumulative "pictures in our heads" about other countries and cultures.

What people in the USSR know about the United States and vice versa is largely a result of the media and other products of popular culture. Since the end of World War II and during the entire period of the Cold War, mostly negative images of the other superpower prevailed in the mass media of these two countries. Images most often reflected each other's foreign policy, officially in the Soviet Union because the press is closely connected with the state and party structure, and indirectly in the United States, where the media—in spite of their presumed adversarial role—have been largely sympathetic to government policies, especially those that are international in character.

The extent to which cognition, attitudes, and behavior are influenced by the content of the media is a matter of considerable conjecture among social scientists and historians, but it is generally agreed that they do play an important role in shaping images, whether alone or in concert with other institutions of society.

In a period when official relations between the United States and the Soviet Union have undergone great change, allowing for warmer and more generous mutual images, it is especially useful to understand what each side thinks of and knows about the other. Although the Soviet and American media differ in their underlying philosophies and ideologies, not to mention their structure and operations, both yield images of the other in their coverage and content.

In recognition of the fact that media images both reflect and guide what people in one country think of those in other nations, a bilateral conference on "Images of the USSR in the United States and the USA in the Soviet Union" was convened at Moscow State University in June and July of 1989. Several American media scholars joined Soviet colleagues, as well as colleagues from the People's Republic of China, in several days of discussions about how the media of the two principal superpowers were portraying one another. Images from news and information outlets as well as those from entertainment were discussed and debated. Scholarly papers were presented and, on occasion, media professionals either joined in or hosted the media scholars in their offices. The purpose of the conference was to foster understanding of existing images of the United States in the USSR and vice versa, as well as to suggest pathways for future cooperation both in academic research and in professional and scholarly exchanges.

The conference was held as the Soviet Union was experiencing extraordinary change in its media system resulting from the government-enunciated policy of glasnost (openness), which has special implications for the press and other communication media, and perestroika (economic restructuring), a concept that also has great domestic economic implications in the Soviet Union. These policies triggered governmental, party, and media changes for Soviet allies and adversaries. Transformations in the Soviet Union, although mostly inspired by the new party and governmental leadership, have altered news media portrayals of the United States in the USSR. Typically, this has meant not only an increase in coverage but more favorable coverage of Americans and their institutions in the Soviet press. In the United States, economic and technological forces, as well as a thaw in official governmental policies, also inspired increased press coverage of the Soviet Union, now regarded as more newsworthy by the U.S. press. The American media also began to cast a more favorable light on the people and policies of the Soviet Union, and especially on its leader, Mikhail Gorbachev.

The several summit meetings between U.S. Presidents Bush and Reagan with Soviet President Gorbachev were lightning rods for news coverage as well as opportunities to reconsider mutual electronic media images whether in the news, entertainment programs, or commercials. Since Mr. Gorbachev came to power and popularized the concepts of glasnost and perestroika, there has been increased interest in each other on both sides of what used to be called the "iron curtain." The winds of change in the USSR and the United States have greatly altered the Cold War. Thus the Moscow conference in summer 1989 was especially timely. It was a forum for an up-to-date report on "mutual images," as well as a detailed look at how these images have been shaped and what they mean to the media systems of both countries. Some of the reported images revealed new attitudes and outlooks, whereas others reflected a long-standing legacy of caution and suspicion. Conferees at the Moscow meetings considered both the enthusiastic expectations prevalent in the summer of 1989 and actual changes in media images, which were quite different. They also debated the term *Cold War* as a communications phenomenon—how it got started, the role of the media in fueling its continuation, and the recent changes that have caused many to challenge the viability and appropriateness of the term to describe the relationship between our two countries. The conferees debated whether the Cold War is completely over or only experiencing a seasonal thaw—a transitional period when we can safely talk about the beginning of the end to this dark time in history.

Whatever name is eventually agreed upon in the debate over changes in mutual images of our two countries, in addition to Europe and the Third World, it is clear that our media merit careful study by scholars in assessing both substantive content and the overt and subtle impact on individuals, institutions, and whole societies. Such study would lead to a better understanding of prevailing media images, attitudes, and values associated with the Cold War.

This volume brings together research papers and essays commissioned for the Moscow conference, largely presented by Soviet and American scholars (as well as colleagues from China). Some additional commentaries by journalists from the two superpowers are also included. The result is a rare mix of integrated voices representing several cultures and modes of presentation, but all fixed on the topic of mutual images and their connection to the end of the Cold War. The reader will find historical analyses of Soviet-American bilateral relations generally and of media relations specifically. Research that examines media content, including general coverage as well as specific events such as summits, is included along with broader studies of the structure and operations of the two media systems. The scholarship here is both documentary and empirical as it examines the present state of images in the respective media systems. Some of the chapters are speculative as they move beyond the recent past and present. Some are bold; others are more cautious. They lead quite naturally to a challenging discussion of future research agendas.

In the end, mutual media images will be the best barometer of success or failure in dismantling the Cold War. At the same time, the media ought not be passive instruments, simply relaying information, but should take a leadership role, instructing and influencing viewers, listeners, and readers. The chapters that follow take advantage of an unparalleled opportunity for scholarly interchange and cooperation. This book, which uniquely draws on the efforts of leading scholars and journalists, is being published simulta- neously in the Soviet Union, the United States, and elsewhere in the world.

Although this book was born at a conference in Moscow, much of its development and execution was done by and at the Gannett Center for Media Studies, now the Gannett Foundation Media Center, in New York City. Martha FitzSimon was significant in developmental editing and making the project whole. Donna Lee Van Cott and Penny Panoulias were involved in editing. To these persons, and to the Center and its parent Gannett Founda- tion, the editors of this volume are deeply grateful.

Everette E. Dennis, New York City
George Gerbner, Philadelphia
Yassen N. Zassoursky, Moscow

Introduction

In 1989 and 1990, on both sides of what Winston Churchill called the "iron curtain," there was much speculation about the impending collapse of the "Cold War," the ominous term used to describe the state of relations between the Soviet Union and the United States roughly since the end of World War II, when the two nations briefly had been allies in that great armed conflict.

The popular media both in the United States and Soviet Union as well as Europe have been awash with articles asking, "Is the Cold War over?" Discussions of the Cold War were not simply journalistic or scholarly speculations but central to statecraft and international relations as well. At the first-ever joint news conference of Soviet and American chiefs of state, itself an indicator of dramatic, new relationships, President Mikhail Gorbachev was asked about President George Bush's call for "an end to the Cold War once and for all." The Soviet leader responded as follows:

> In the first place, I assured the President of the United States that the Soviet Union would never start "hot war" against the United States of America. And, we would like our relations to develop in such a way that they would open greater possibilities for cooperation. Naturally, the President and I had a wide discussion, where we sought the answer to the question of where we stand now. We stated, both of us, that the world leaves one epoch of Cold War, and enters another epoch. This is just the beginning. We are just at the very beginning of our road, long road to a long-lasting, peaceful period. (*Washington Post,* December 4, 1989, p. A22; *Pravda* and *Izvestia,* December 5, pp. 1-2)

Whether the worldwide ideological struggle was on hold, only slowing, or genuinely moving to a conclusion was the subject of hundreds of articles in scores of languages in the 1980s, a trend likely to continue in the 1990s.

The concept of the "Cold War" is so institutionalized that it even won an entry in *The American Dictionary of the English Language* as "a state of political tension and military rivalry between nations, stopping short of actual full-scale war" (1970, p. 260). More specifically, it had come to mean the rivalries between the United States and the USSR as well as those nations within their respective spheres of influence, especially in Europe after World War II. The Cold War also extended to "client states" and allies of the two superpowers in Latin America, Africa, and Asia. Although both "sides" built up massive nuclear stockpiles, amassed troops on both sides in Europe and elsewhere, and justified military interventions in the Third World, the only

1

war between the two superpowers was a war of words, characterized by bellicose rhetoric. Although the Cold War has certainly been marked by such "real" factors as economic aid to neutral nations as well as client states, it has been largely a communications phenomenon wherein the "war" was carried out in activities variously called public information, propaganda, or disinformation, depending on one's ideology or interpretation. Though we assume that some of the "communications war" involved espionage—encouraged, ignited, and monitored by the respective security establishments—this book is concerned with mutual images, those combinations of shadows and light, text and visualization, created and channeled by the mass media, rather than other matters of foreign policy or military relations.

What is the Cold War?

In media discussions of the current state of the Cold War (whether it has ended, is ending, or is pausing), Saul Pett of the Associated Press called the Cold War "a surreal struggle fed by mutual fear." As he put it, "For nearly half a century, nearly a fifth of the life of the American republic, two giants have terrified each other astride a world they held in thrall with their power and enmity" (*AP Newsfeatures Report,* August 7, 1989, p. 1). The Cold War was played out in the media as a contest between the two superpowers.

No one can be certain just when and where the Cold War started. Typically, it is described as a post-World War II phenomenon, but it would be naive to suggest that a warm policy of mutual trust existed between the two countries in the preceding decades. The United States had "red scares" in the years before and after World War I, when a fear of Bolshevik forces stirred considerable controversy in the public press and inspired espionage statutes. On the Soviet side there was considerable fear of and hostility toward the Americans and other Cold War participants. Similar sentiments in the United States arose during the Great Depression of the 1930s when leftist movements in this country looked to Moscow and Marxist-Leninist thought for guidance. This and other ideological conflicts and doubts about the American system faded during World War II when the nation joined in a crusade to defeat Germany and Japan. At that time the Soviet Union was an ally of the United States and even benefited from the Lend-Lease program. Immediately after the war, the future of Europe and issues relating to the security of atomic secrets brought suspicion and a "war of words" to relations between the two countries. From the American perspective the Cold War emerged and was guided by a policy of containment, originally advanced by the master diplomat George F. Kennan in 1946 and 1947. This was seconded and reinforced in speeches by President Harry Truman, in which he enunciated his Truman Doctrine, and in Winston Churchill's "iron curtain" speech. The policy of containment, articulated by Kennan, has in various incarnations guided all American administrations from Harry Truman to George Bush. The Cold War was, of course, a conflict between communism and capitalism with each side defending the virtuous features of its system while denouncing the other as its principal adversary. The two nations that entered World War II as important, but not dominant, world powers would dominate the postmodern world as they sought to spread their influence. Just how that was done and with what relative success was seen as the two countries expanded their spheres of direct and indirect control not only in Europe, but also in Africa, Asia, and Latin America. The Cold War largely defined international policy for the superpowers as well as other nations who could seek support and even manipulate the United States and the USSR in the process.

From a standpoint of international communication, the Cold War governed the flow of information both in the control of foreign correspondents in their respective societies and in the availability of information between and among the two sides and their allies.

From an American perspective, the Cold War was the result of a decline of trust almost immediately after World War II. After considerable Soviet expansion during and subsequent to the war, including both the consolidation of the Soviet republics and alliances with (or domination of) the Warsaw Pact nations of Eastern Europe, the United States could boast that its containment policies had been mostly successful from the Berlin blockade of the 1940s to the installation of U.S. intermediate range nuclear missiles in Europe in the 1980s. Commentators spoke of the Americans as having "won" the Cold War in Europe while "losing" in China, Cuba, and a few other locations. In some regions of the world, Western-style governments and parties competed fiercely with Marxist-Leninist regimes and political factions.

Third World Communications

In a real sense, the Third World, much of it made up of former colonies of the West (Britain, France, Germany, Spain, Portugal, etc.), was a staging ground for East-West conflict in the Middle East, black Africa, Central and South America, and South Asia, with both the Soviets and the Americans offering economic aid as they advised governments, supported military operations, and sold their ideologies in direct and covert ways. Some Third

World nations are heavily dependent on superpower aid that has been given largely to stave off the rival's ideology and influence over future governmental policies. By the 1990s, the Soviet Union, with domestic economic problems and considerable internal dissension, had less reason to support activities in some countries; especially those in Latin America, according to a 1989 study by the Council on Foreign Relations. The United States, with deficits and economic shortcomings that make massive foreign aid less attractive, is watching warily for pullbacks of Soviet commitments, which might just be a rationale for a diminution of U.S. resources as well. The United States also faces a dilemma wherein its moral support for greater independence in the Baltic states and Eastern Europe cannot be accompanied with much foreign aid—either economic or military—without cutbacks elsewhere in the world, including, for example, the Middle East, where billions of dollars flow to Israel and Egypt. Such a scenario might mean that one of the consequences of the 1980s debate over the Cold War might be felt as deeply in the Third World, because it is less useful (and less vital) to respective American and Soviet interests.

The Cold War: Essentially a European Affair

To the Western media, the Cold War has always been seen in terms of winners and losers. The failure of Eurocommunism to gain control of governments in Italy and France, for example, was a "win" for the West, while the Red Army victory over the Nationalists in China was a "defeat." Sometimes there were ambivalent interpretations—as in Berlin, where the Berlin airlift succeeded but the creation of the Berlin Wall was regarded as a stalemate for both sides. It was at once an assertion of territoriality by the East Germans and a symbol of a frustrated totalitarian state from a West German perspective. It was assumed, of course, that Soviet and U.S. interests were driving forces on both sides of the Wall.

One useful perspective on the Cold War was offered by *Newsweek* in an issue of the magazine that declared, "The Cold War is Over." *Newsweek* identified a chronology of five key dates that helped define the Cold War, for Americans at least:

   1950—The Cold War spawns a regional conflict: Communist soldiers of the Korean People's Army are in combat.
   1956—Moscow's *cordon sanitaire:* Hungarians try to topple the Stalinists, but Soviet tanks crush the rebellion.
   1961—Before the "common European home": To stem the westward flood of East Germans, Nikita Khrushchev built the Berlin Wall.

1962—At the edge of oblivion: President Kennedy's men huddle outside the White House during the Cuban missile crisis.
1968—Mean wars in the Third World: America intervenes in Vietnam and finds itself unable to defeat Hanoi's communist forces.

Whereas such a chronology focuses mainly on international dilemmas, at home in the United States an ideology of the Cold War was regularly reinforced in congressional investigations and their prominent play in the media. From the late 1940s on, such investigations of "un-American activities," which were defined as "aiding and abetting the communists," brought film stars, intellectuals, literary figures, and government officials before committees and cameras, perhaps peaking in the famed McCarthy hearings of 1950-1954. These hearings ignited the "red scare" of that period called McCarthyism, named for the sleuthing Wisconsin senator who was later discredited in television assaults on his own hearings, especially in broadcasts by Edward R. Murrow of CBS. Although McCarthyism faded by the mid-1950s, occasional recurrences of anticommunist activism would return in conservative political movements in the late 1950s and finally find voice in the nomination of Barry Goldwater for the Republican presidential nomination in 1964. Many of the values expressed in that campaign would be carried forth by Richard Nixon (who first gained fame as a "red-hunter"), and then by Ronald Reagan when he was elected to the presidency in 1980 and reelected in 1984. Indeed, it was President Reagan who voiced the "evil empire" metaphor to describe the Soviet Union in 1983, only to pull back from this after developing summit initiatives with the Soviets in 1988.

Occasionally, there were thaws in U.S.-Soviet relations, notably during the administrations of Dwight Eisenhower (1953-1961) and subsequently during the Nixon administration in the late 1960s and early 1970s when a policy of détente was initiated.

The media often mirrored public attitudes toward the Soviet Union and the prevailing U.S. policy; however, educational and cultural exchanges between the two countries were inconsistent and infrequent, with official and unofficial relations often being marked by suspicion and hostility. In general, during much of this period—as subsequent chapters of this book indicate—mostly negative images of the other country and people prevailed on both sides. News reporting usually was a transmission belt for the heated rhetoric of the two protagonists, often as they denounced each other in such forums as the United Nations. During this period, both countries carefully controlled the number of journalists admitted from the other side and were not reluctant to expel reporters with little notice or formal charge. Such a policy echoed in both countries did little to foster a free flow of information, let alone enhance public understanding of each other.

A Time of Transition

From the mid-1980s on, new directions in Soviet policy, especially as enunciated in the concepts of perestroika (economic restructuring) and glasnost (openness), were viewed with cautious optimism in the West. From a communications perspective, dramatic changes in Soviet information policy were evident from the time of the nuclear accident at Chernobyl in April 1986. For the first time in Western memory, Soviet television and other media reported on the accident openly and with dispatch. Although Western media typically have emphasized negative news, even when it embarrassed their own governments, this was not common in the Soviet Union. This, accompanied by President Gorbachev's personal public style and use of television, was noticed almost immediately in the United States and elsewhere. Commentators asked whether it signaled a change in policy and what the impact might be on the release and flow of information generally, the role of the Soviet media, and the practices of journalists and other information disseminators.

For the West, at least, answers came in the several summit meetings when President Gorbachev met first with President Reagan in Iceland, Washington, and Moscow, and then with President Bush in Malta and Washington. In these encounters and in concurrent meetings of foreign ministers, military officials, and others, words and deeds were closely observed. Discussions of the reduction of nuclear armaments and arms in Europe were most significant as it became clear that both sides, notably prodded first by the Soviets, were changing their policies while still keeping a wary eye on each other.

Communications have been central to the waning of the Cold War, with U.S. and Soviet leaders appearing uncensored on television in their respective countries, greater freedom for broadcast and print media in covering each other's affairs, spacebridges linking American and Soviet commentators and citizen groups in telecommunication linkups, and other signs of a thaw.

As Admiral William J. Crowe, chairman of the U.S. Joint Chiefs of Staff, said to an audience at the Soviet Academy of Sciences, "We are literally members of a transitional generation." One of the characteristics of this transitional period has been the tendency of the two sides to deny each other the status of being "its main enemy," in the words of foreign policy expert Stanley Hoffman of Harvard University. Defining our respective worlds in terms of conflict and contest has provided a simplified, even if potentially dangerous, way of relating to each other. It was an understandable way to carve up the world and to communicate to mass audiences. In our news presentations and popular culture representations, both countries depicted the other as the enemy, sometimes in demonic terms. The novelist Gore Vidal has said that communications in the present transitional period is often "good television one-upmanship" wherein post-Cold War "winners and losers" will be those that triumph on television, projecting the most sympathetic and positive image. Vidal and other critics think that television has played a key role in the United States and the USSR "demonizing" each other. Vidal asked rhetorically of his own country, "What will the United States do without The Enemy?—a pretty daring question from those whose livelihood depends on the demonizing of Russia and Communism." Others might substitute "America and capitalism."

The transitional period ought not be seen in simplistic terms, for it is more than diplomatic initiatives and foreign policy/defense outcomes with Europe and the Third World as staging grounds. It is a redefinition of how two traditional enemies look at each other and the rest of the world. It will be strongly tied to developments in the Soviet republics and in the states of Eastern Europe that were complex formulations involving changes in governments and party alignments as well as ethnic identities. Linkages between the Europe of the West and the Europe of the East, overcoming always artificial barriers created by wars and revolutions over several centuries, will also define the new relationships and convergences of understandings between and among peoples.

The present climate of cooperation between the Soviet Union and the United States is often seen in very recent terms, mainly dating to 1985, but this is misleading. There has not been a monolithic Cold War since the end of World War II. There have, of course, been dark periods of hard-line separation, but there have been diplomatic relations constantly since 1933, when Franklin Roosevelt sent his first ambassador to Moscow and the Soviet government reciprocated.

After a limited alliance during World War II, the two countries threatened each other again and again from the 1940s through the 1980s, although many experts thought that nuclear stockpiles on both sides made a "hot war" unlikely. Still, events in Germany, Hungary, Czechoslovakia, Korea, Vietnam, Afghanistan, Cuba, and elsewhere, had the two great powers issuing threats and demands that could have erupted into armed conflict. And indeed, both countries have been suppliers of economic and military aid to a continuing series of small wars and conflicts on several continents since the 1950s. These interventions, although short of war, were surrogates for actual combat between our two societies. During the 40 years of the Cold War, diplomatic summits sometimes promised hope for a period of warmth and cooperation. For example, the summits involving President Khrushchev and Presidents Eisenhower and Kennedy, although sometimes stormy, led to various artistic, cultural, and scientific exchanges.

Always there seemed to be great expectations and false starts interrupted by hostile acts and misunderstandings. In the early 1960s, the downing of an American spy plane in the Soviet Union spelled the end to closer relations. Later, Soviet involvement in Cuba and a showdown in front of television cameras at the United Nations gave fuel to the Cold War and even threatened a hot one. During some of the same period, the deepening U.S. involvement in Vietnam, the "living room war," cast images of death and dying around the world. A similar condition would exist with the Soviet involvement in Afghanistan in the 1980s. The U.S. boycott of the Olympic games, the off-and-on trade agreements between the two countries, the downing of a Korean Air Lines plane, and other international incidents did more than their share to keep the Cold War alive.

Ironically, from an American perspective it was Richard Nixon, a dedicated anticommunist, who opened a new era of détente in the early 1970s when he and President Brezhnev met in summit meetings in both the United States and the Soviet Union. Scholars now look back on this once-promising period as fostering "a misleading exchange of misunderstandings." Still, during that period there was once again a climate for exchange and cooperation, a climate that would be rekindled in the 1980s.

Most commentators from a variety of ideological perspectives agree that it was both the communications strategies and the personal style of Mikhail Gorbachev that most significantly signaled the new understanding and yearning for an end to the Cold War that emerged in the 1980s. Although this has been perhaps the most visible indication of a new attitude on both sides, any support for an end to the Cold War has come from a diverse set of factors, some involving governments and policy changes initiated and implemented by scores of people and institutions, others connected to economic realities and both a new form of economic socialism in the Soviet Union and a desire by the USSR to become part of the world system of economic and currency exchanges. On both sides a willingness to consider, even cautiously, new relationships and new understandings has required cooperation and compromise.

Considerations for Communication

Throughout this period the media have been barometers for relative thaws and chills in the diplomatic, social, and cultural atmosphere. Sometimes communications have changed slowly with cautious, critical, and sometimes misleading language being used to describe summits and the respective conditions in the two countries. At our bilateral media studies meetings in

Moscow in June 1989, Soviet observers moaned disapprovingly at U.S. television portrayals (then being shown) of their country, while Americans responded in like manner when Washington, DC, was portrayed in the grimmest terms by Soviet commentators.

Still, as the events of 1989 in China, Eastern Europe, and the Soviet Union have indicated, something new is in the air. Although these events and actions may be portrayed and perceived differently in the Soviet Union than in the United States, they do mark a new era of communications in which international communications have succeeded in shrinking the world's distances and discontinuities into a global village.

For media scholars and professional communicators, our perceptions of changes on both sides—in real events, responses and formal policies, and material actions—will not be enhanced if they are simply described in terms of winners and losers. Although some in the West see the decline of the Cold War as a period of great opportunity for cooperation (and friendly competition), others see it simply as a failure of one system in favor of the other and talk in terms of "winning" the Cold War. Such a notion is antithetical to any real end of the old tensions of the Cold War, which will require trust—largely through communications at first and real actions later. For scholars, moralizing about winning and losing will not effectuate understanding of any similarities and mutual cooperation between two very different peoples, cultures, and operational systems.

The end of the Cold War offers an opportunity for more systematic, scholarly study of the communication systems of the two respective cultures and of the rest of the world. Although this volume is dedicated to an American-Soviet exchange with commentary from Chinese media scholars, future research ventures might contemplate true international and multinational scholarship. Similarly, at the level of media operations, various exchanges that have been ongoing for some time could be advanced and developed so that cooperation on news, entertainment, and opinion ventures could be commonplace rather than rare.

If there is to be a new American-Soviet communications alliance, it has to have the potential to provide leadership for the rest of the world, not as a hostile competitor, but as an expediter for new ventures between quite different traditions whether in scholarship, media work, public opinion, or other aspects of modern international communication.

To these goals this volume is dedicated as a new beginning among scholars and their colleagues, who are not strangers to each other nor to each other's systems, but individuals representing institutions whose societies have much to gain in fostering and fashioning new, productive relationships. They are not so naive as to think that universal agreement will be the result—for we are by nature competitive and quite different systems—but they recognize that the idea of mutual benefit can have far-reaching effects.

E.E.D.
G.G.
Y.N.Z.

1
Changing Images of the Soviet Union and the United States

YASSEN N. ZASSOURSKY

The history of the exchange of information between the United States and the Soviet Union is more than 300 years old. The first articles about America were published in Russia in the late seventeenth century, at about the same time the American press began creating its image of Russia. Through all these years there was only one era during which the images of the Soviet Union and the United States became outspokenly negative: the period of the Cold War.

Russia has always evinced great interest in America. The first reports from America in the seventeenth and eighteenth centuries were devoted to the life of American natives, whereas later writings focused on the American Revolution. Russian authors sympathized with the Indians, disapproving of the white settlers' virtual annihilation of the Indian tribes. The Russian members of the Enlightenment, beginning with Alexander N. Radishchev, hailed the war for independence and were positive and mostly enthusiastic in their treatment of the activities of George Washington, Thomas Jefferson, and Benjamin Franklin. Russian authors were of course worried about the new problems that appeared in the young American republic, in particular the domination of mercantilism. Vissarion G. Belinsky, for example, recognized in James Fenimore Cooper's writings a passionate protest against mercantilism and expressed his own concern on the subject.

In nineteenth-century Russia special attention was focused on the struggle against the enslavement of black Americans. The Russian authors who fought against serfdom in Russia had a great deal of respect for the writings of abolitionists. Henry Wadsworth Longfellow's *Songs of Slavery* was widely circulated in Russia. Harriet Beecher Stowe's *Uncle Tom's Cabin* was translated into Russian and immediately became a best-seller. The progressive people of Russia applauded the victory of the North over the Southern slave owners.

In comparison, Russia aroused less interest from the United States, at least during its early history. Joel Barlow, an American poet who was dispatched to Russia on a diplomatic mission to negotiate with Napoleon, was one of the first to write about Russia. Just before his death in Russia in December of 1812, he wrote a poem that became famous: "Advice to the Raven in Russia," in which the realities of Russian society were represented in the image of the Russian frost. Because the frost did not allow the raven to capture its prey or to deal with frozen corpses, the poet advised the raven:

> Fly then or starve: though all the dreadful Road
> From Minsk to Moscow with their bodies strowed
> May count some myriads, yet they can't suffice
> To feed you more beneath these dreary skies.
> Go back, and winter in the wilds of Spain.
> (*The Oxford Book of American Verse*, selected and with an introduction by J. O. Matthiessen, Oxford University Press, 1957, p. 49).

To Barlow, Napoleon was a tyrant whose deeds deserved denunciation and who would be hurled from his blood-built throne, this king of woes: "Dash him to dust, and let the world repose" (*Oxford Book of American Verse*, 1957, p. 49). Barlow did not specifically reveal his attitude toward Russia, but his condemnation of Napoleon and his view of the Russian battlefield implied compassion for the Russian people.

The great American poet Walt Whitman expressed a then-popular understanding of the relations between Russia and America in a letter dated December 20, 1881, to Dr. John Fitzgerald Lee of Trinity College in Dublin, who had asked Whitman's permission to translate his poetry into Russian. Whitman said there were not only differences but, more than that, there was coincidence in the character of Russians and Americans, and that many traits of the two countries were very similar. Whitman's view is still apparent in the thinking of many Russians and Americans:

> You Russians and we Americans—our countries so distant, so unlike at first glance—such a difference in social and political conditions, and our respective methods of moral and practical development the last hundred years; and yet in certain features, and vastest ones, so resembling each other. The variety of stock-elements and tongues to be resolutely fused in a common identity and union at all hazards—the idea, perennial through the ages, that they both have their historic and divine mission—the fervent element of manly friendship—throughout the whole people, surpassed by no other races—the grand expanse of territorial limits and boundaries—the unformed and nebulous state of many things, not yet permanently settled, but agreed on all hands to be the preparations

of an infinitely greater future—the fact that both peoples have their independent and leading positions to hold, keep and if necessary fight for, against the rest of the world—the deathless aspirations at the inmost centre of each great community, so vehement, so mysterious, so abysmic—are certainly features you Russians and we Americans possess in common. (*Walt Whitman, The Correspondence,* edited by E. H. Miller, 1969, p. 259)

These words reflect the images of Russia and America that were being formulated by the end of the nineteenth century. The American image of Russia was based on the concept of the mysteriousness of the Russian soul. The similarities between the Russian and American frontiers united these countries, giving them a sense of parallel uniqueness, grandeur, and a sense of mission. The Russians felt a closeness with the souls and characters of Americans, especially in contrast to their feelings about the Europeans whose countries were divided by internal and intrastate strifes and composed of smaller territories. As illustrated by Walt Whitman's letter, Americans had a similar understanding of Russians.

Even today these images dwell in the depths of the national and popular thinking of our countries and engender a mutual sympathy between our peoples regardless of changes in the political climate. The Cold War drove this climate to the freezing point but never arrived at the stage of military confrontation, with the exception of an American military presence for intervention purposes against Soviet Russia in 1918-1920 in the Far East and the north of Russia.

The progressive people of America supported the progressive people of Russia in their struggle against the czarist regime. Mark Twain published his essay "The Czar's Soliloquy" in March 1905 in the *North American Review,* in which he criticized the czar and czarism and expressed strong opposition to the czar's dictatorship. Twain expressed his sympathy for the Russian revolution in a speech presented at a New York club where he shared the platform with Maxim Gorky.

A similar sentiment was expressed by John Reed, a journalist who became closely involved in the events of the great October Revolution. His book, *Ten Days That Shook the World,* became one of the main sources for historians of the Russian revolution, generating vivid images of the revolution in the United States and throughout the world. Reed and others helped spur America's admiration of the revolutionary energy of the Soviet people.

But Reed and his writings represented only one facet of American perceptions of events in Russia; others held different views. Robert Wilton wrote his book *The Agony of Russia* in 1919; Arthur Bullard published *The Russian Revolution Pendulum: Autocracy, Democracy, Bolshevism* that same year;

and Edgar Sisson compiled a 1918 pamphlet entitled "German Bolshevik Conspiracy" (*War Information Series,* issued by the Committee on Public Information, Washington, 1918) in which Sisson forged a false version of Lenin's biography and tried to present him as a German spy. D. R. Francis published another book of the same caliber and character, *Russia from the American Embassy,* in 1921. These books started the tradition of anti-Sovietism in American writing against which there was subsequent opposition, especially from writers of the realist school.

A group of American intellectuals published *Civilization in the United States: An Inquiry by Thirty Americans,* edited by Harold E. Stearns (1922). This book contained John Macy's article "Journalism," which strongly denounced the anti-Sovietism of the American press and challenged the bases of several critical books. Although I do not wish to say that these books lacked any factual bases, Lenin stated in a letter to American workers in August 1918 that anti-Soviet propaganda was spreading widely in the Western world: "Let the corrupt bourgeois press shout to the whole world every mistake our revolution makes. We are not daunted by our mistakes. People have not become saints because the revolution has begun" (V. I. Lenin, *Collected Works,* Volume 28, Progress Publishers, Moscow, 1965, pp. 71-72).

In my opinion, these mistakes were used by the bourgeois press in the United States to create a false picture of the revolution and of revolutionary reality. Later, John Macy, Walter Lippmann, and other more objective American researchers brought these mistakes to the attention of world opinion.

Overall we can trace three tendencies in the American evaluation of the October Revolution. One was an acceptance of John Reed's view, that of encouraging the revolution; another was clearly anti-Soviet. A third tendency was that of authors who tried to be objective in their assessment of the revolution but did not accept the revolutionary thesis of the Bolsheviks. I would include in this category Colonel Raymond Robins, head of the American Red Cross in Russia, whose impressions of Soviet Russia were published in *Raymond Robins's Impressions as Told to William Hard* (1920). These three interpretative theories dominated American literature about Russia until the early 1930s. At that time a new interest in Soviet Russia arose in the United States as a result of the establishment of diplomatic relations between the two countries by President Franklin Delano Roosevelt, who played an important role in the development of Soviet-American relations.

The 1930s are known in American literature as the Red (or Rosy or Pink) Decade. Practically every known and read American author of that period was fascinated by Soviet Russia. Earlier, in the 1920s, Theodore Dreiser and John Dos Passos had visited Soviet Russia, and their impressions of the country fostered a new vision of life in the Soviet Union.

Soviet-American relations reached a new peak during World War II, after some cooling connected with the Soviet-German nonaggression pact and the Soviet-Finnish war. During World War II, Soviet writers were widely published in the United States, where their books sold briskly. Constantin Simonov's novel *Days and Nights* was on the best-seller list in the early 1940s. Hollywood produced films about the Soviet Union with considerable success at the box office. Those films were certainly creating a much more sympathetic image of Soviets—the Soviet Union generally and especially the Soviet people. The allied Soviet-American struggle against fascism during World War II resurrected the traditions of the friendship of the two peoples predicted by Walt Whitman.

After the October Revolution, the Russian attitude toward America was developing in different directions as well. Vladimir Lenin's previously mentioned letter to American workers stated:

> Bourgeois civilization has borne all its luxurious fruits. America has taken first place among the free and educated nations in the level of development of the productive forces of collective United Human endeavor, in the utilization of machinery and of all the wonders of modern engineering. At the same time, America has become one of the foremost countries in regard to the depth of the abyss which lies between the handful of arrogant multimillionaires who wallow in filth and luxury, and the millions of working people who constantly live on the verge of pauperism. (V. I. Lenin, *Collected Works,* 1965, pp. 62-63)

Lenin's words were the key to the image of America that then dominated Soviet journalism and writing. There was considerable enthusiasm for the wonders of the newest and most modern technology, the leader among the free and educated peoples, the highest level of the development of free creative and productive resources and human labor. Even so, there were the contradictions of poverty and the evils of bourgeois civilization. The world economic crisis of 1929 proved Lenin's thesis. The poverty of the unemployed and the collapse of many American enterprises were described in detail by American newspapers and magazines. American writers and journalists were anxious to find the cause of this tragic situation in their country. Their articles, books, and stories were widely reprinted by the Soviet newspapers and contributed to the description of the contradictions and tragedies of the Great Depression in the United States.

At the same time in the Soviet Union a new attitude toward America was gaining popularity: an appeal to learn to work in the American way. The idea was that the Soviet people should combine the Russian revolutionary scope and spirit with American business ability. This new interest in America and

Americans that was developing in the Soviet Union in the 1920s and 1930s was reflected in the well-known and very popular book by Ilya and Evgeniy Petrov, *One Story America* (1936), which they wrote after traveling throughout the United States. In 1933 Samuel Marshak, a leading Soviet poet who wrote especially for children, published his poem "Mister Twister" in which he described the travels of an American businessman in the Soviet Union. Although Marshak was critical of Soviet hotels and their service, he was ironic about the attitude of the American businessman, and his poem was characteristic of the attitude toward America at this time. American businessmen as well as laborers were frequent visitors to the Soviet Union in the 1930s to participate in the construction of many important industrial enterprises, including the Gorky automobile factory. At the same time, Soviet workers went to the United States to study the methods of modern technology and management. The treatment of American capitalism in Soviet writing about the United States often was quite critical, superficial, and loud, but also had an element of admiration. Soviet writings about the American people were generally positive, characterized by respect for their business acumen, technical genius, and managerial achievements.

World War II contributed to the strengthening and reinforcement of mutual sympathies. Although the rhetoric used to describe the relationship of the two countries had changed to the language of friendship, comaraderie, and cooperation, in some ways it remained on the same level as in the 1930s. For example, the Soviet press reported that American conservatives and business were still suspicious of, if not hostile to, the Soviet Union. The cooling of Soviet-American relations started soon after the end of World War II and quickly reached the stage of the Cold War. One American senator—whose name I do not like even to mention—and his allies in the United States embarked on a fierce anti-Soviet campaign. Although there were many examples of the anti-Soviet publications in the United States during this time, I will mention only one of them to stress its negative effect. The notorious "Red Issue" of *Collier's,* published on October 27, 1951, described a fictitious Moscow occupied by American troops. During that period, the American press was actively promoting a negative image of the Soviets as aggressive, lazy, illiterate, foolish, and uneducated. It was the first time in the history of Soviet-American relations that the image of the Soviet as an enemy was portrayed with such bluntness.

Sputnik, the first Soviet space satellite, which was launched in 1957, proved instrumental in destroying the stereotype of the Soviet brute and in sobering the American attitude. At the same time, the 20th Congress of the Communist Party of the Soviet Union began attempts to revitalize Soviet external and internal policies, starting at the time of the thaw and coinciding with the first attempts at improvement of Soviet-American relations.

But after this first thaw, there came a cooling of the international atmosphere at the end of the 1960s with the war in Vietnam providing grounds for a second wave of the Cold War. An improvement in Soviet-American relations at the beginning of the 1970s warmed relations, but that soon ended with a third wave of the Cold War by the end of the 1970s and early 1980s. This third and strongest wave of the Cold War was reflected in President Ronald Reagan's portrayal of the Soviet Union as "an evil empire" in his speech before the British Parliament in March 1983. One of the extremes of the American anti-Soviet propaganda was demonstrated by a book, *What Will Happen to You When the Soviets Take Over?* (edited by Ingo Swann, Scarform, Inc., Belmont, CA, 1980). It essentially was a revision of the "Red Issue" of *Collier's,* filled with animosity toward the Soviet Union.

Soviet journalism of the Cold War period criticized American imperialism, which was treated as the main source of international reaction. The Soviet journalists' confrontational style contributed to the creation of new stereotypes and trite phrases like the "sharks of imperialism." The most explicit anti-Americanism was found in caricatures published by the Soviet popular satirical magazine, *Krokodil (The Crocodile).* American researchers who studied these stereotypes determined that *Krokodil* divided Americans into two categories: the poor, lean, and exploited ordinary people fighting for peace, and the fat capitalists who smoked cigars and prepared for World War III.

After the 20th Congress of the Communist Party of the Soviet Union, these stereotypes underwent substantial change. Soviet journalists who accompanied Nikita Sergeivich Khrushchev on his trip to the United States published a book, *Face to Face With America,* in which they tried to alter the images and stereotypes and were in many ways successful. They deserved acclaim for that book and were in fact awarded the Lenin Prize. The confrontational style continued to appear in Soviet publications as new waves of the Cold War rolled in, but it continued in a weakened form and never reached the level of ferocity achieved in earlier decades.

A new period in Soviet-American relations began after the Geneva meeting of the leaders of the two countries, when President Reagan and Secretary General Mikhail Gorbachev met. The new political thinking promoted by Gorbachev underscored the need to destroy the enemy image, to disregard the old confrontational style, and to foster a partnership more in keeping with the interdependency of the world. The dramatic changes in Soviet-American relations after 1985 affected the entire world.

American mass media also made serious efforts to end the old enemy stereotypes of the Soviet Union and present a more reasonable and objective image. Especially notable was American television's coverage of the U.S.-USSR summit meeting in Moscow in 1988. America was broadcasting pictures from Red Square, the Kremlin, Royssia Hotel and Spago House, the residence of the American ambassador in Moscow. These direct broadcasts led to a real change in the American public's perception of the Soviet Union. In the past, the Red Square and the Kremlin were the symbols of the "red menace" and the embodiment of the "evil empire," used for American anti-Soviet propaganda. But the American broadcasts showed a much different and more realistic image of Soviet institutions. The broadcasts from the Hotel Royssia and from Moscow streets presented the Soviet Union in a new and more compassionate light. This was a great achievement for American television, although even these broadcasts were often marred by Cold War rhetoric and a somewhat confrontational tone, particularly in the judgments, evaluations, and conclusions of commentators.

In addition to television, the print media also began to shift toward a more objective approach toward the Soviet Union. In April 1989, *Time* magazine published a special issue, "The New USSR," which expressed a new approach to the Soviet Union and was quite successful in changing attitudes and transcending the confrontational approach previously characteristic of *Time*'s attitude toward the Soviet Union.

Nevertheless, it is a pity that even today we can find remnants of the Cold War. For example, the well-known publishing house of McGraw-Hill published Martin Ebon's *The Soviet Propaganda Machine* (1987). Another prominent publishing house, Dodd Mead and Company, published a book titled *Mesmerized by the Bear: The Soviet Strategy of Deception* (1987), which warned the American public not to trust Gorbachev or to support perestroika. I must say that it is difficult to find analogies in the Soviet press. Although some Soviet publications still contain confrontational elements, they are for the most part more subtle. But in 1989 the publishing house of the APN news agency issued Karamanov's *American Cultural Invasion* whose front cover pictured Europe in the embrace of the American monster. Unfortunately, the book contains very primitive and preconceived evaluations of American culture.

Although the new political thinking is making good progress, it is also encountering some difficulties. The deadly rhetoric of the Cold War is sometimes poisoning the improved atmosphere of Soviet-American relations. In this connection, I would single out the article published in *Daedalus* (Winter, 1990) and partially reprinted in *The New York Times* ("To the Stalin Mausoleum," January 4, 1990), signed by "Z." The author of this article tries to present a neoconservative vision that goes against improving the relations between the peoples of the two countries and leads to a confrontational analysis of Soviet-American relations. We can only hope that this is one of the last salvos fired in the Cold War. But the practitioners of the Cold

War—the so-called cold warriors—cannot keep silent and are trying to revitalize their technique of confrontation. I sincerely hope that the media of the Soviet Union and of the United States combine their efforts to thwart confrontational thinking, to develop cooperation in solving the global problems that are making our earth smaller every day, and to call attention to the serious task of preserving our planet for the generations to come.

The spirit expressed in Walt Whitman's letter about the Russians exemplifies my hope:

> And as my dearest dream is for an internationality of poems and poets binding the lands of the earth closer than all treaties or diplomacy—as the purpose beneath the best in my book is such hearty comradeship for individuals to begin with, and for all the Nations of the earth as a result—how happy indeed I shall be to get the hearing and emotional contact of the great Russian peoples! (*Walt Whitman, The Correspondence,* edited by E. H. Miller, 1969, p. 259)

Whitman's dreams of contacts between the great peoples of Russia and the United States should be promoted not only by poets, but by the mass media of both countries.

Media and communications researchers have a special role to play. It is up to them to identify and overcome the barriers that prevent the development of information exchanges and to establish real and honest communication between both peoples. It is a difficult task for researchers and it is yet more complicated for the mass media, but the resultant yield will be illuminating and useful in ending the inertia of the Cold War. We can now afford to be optimistic. Our peoples no longer perceive each other as enemies. And the recent developments, the summit meetings of the leaders of the two countries, and the new moves toward demilitarization of Europe are all important contributions to the improvement in the international atmosphere.

The mass media can further this process. Although there are political, trade, and military factors to be considered at this stage of Soviet-American relations, the communication and information aspects are becoming more and more important. Increased knowledge about each other and the objective and truthful images of each other's interests and efforts are becoming more and more urgent. By evaluating the activities of the media, especially during the last five years, we will learn that overcoming the enemy/confrontational image may not be easy but it is possible. Moreover, it is urgently necessary, and the efforts in this direction taken so far by both Soviet and American media are encouraging.

In the end I believe we will learn much from each other because our mutual interests and passions are very deep and very real. We have a variety of ethnic groups and languages that should be understood in holistic fashion. Each of the countries has its own history and a sacred mission is common to both. The passion for heroic friendship has never been expressed with such force as it has been between the United States and the USSR. We have much in common, such as vast riches of land, broadly outlined borders, and the very formlessness and chaotic character of many events of life. We also share a still-unrealized foundation of the unknown and even greater future. These are the factors that bring us together. In addition, we each have an independent leading position in the world that we are trying to keep intact and for which we are both ready to fight the rest of the world. Immortal ills that live in the depths of both great countries—so passionate, so mysterious, so bottomless—all this too is characteristic of Americans and Russians.

Ideally, the images of the two nations should come as close to reality as possible, and this depends upon access to information about reality. Although there has been a noticeable increase in the exchanges of people—both private visitors and tourists—the number of people visiting is still very limited because of the distance, expense, and complications of travel. The only realistic way to close the gap between the two countries is by promoting new and permanent information links. Characteristic of this, one of the first steps in improving Soviet-American relations was the establishment of the "hot line" between the White House and the Kremlin. A similar hot line should be established between the peoples of the two countries: This aim can be achieved only through the creation of a system of information and media interdependence.

2
Images of America

ELLEN MICKIEWICZ

Television is a relatively new but immensely powerful medium of communication. In the last few years the Soviet Union has experienced drastic changes politically and socially, and these changes can be seen in Soviet television. The image of the United States on Soviet television is a particularly significant object of study that has also undergone substantial change over the last few years. Before examining these recent and compelling changes it will be useful to add a historical perspective by examining ways that Russians who came into contact with the United States before 1917 saw America. This was the subject of a fascinating study by Robert V. Allen titled *Russia Looks at America: The View to 1917* (Library of Congress, Washington, DC, 1988). We shall find, I think, that there are some surprising parallels to the present day.

Aleksandr Radishchev, in his seminal work *Journey from Petersburg to Moscow* (1790), specifically praised the provisions of the constitutions of the American states of Pennsylvania, Delaware, Maryland, and Virginia that allowed for freedom of the press. But he also noted that despite protestations of liberty in America, a large part of the population was then made up of black slaves. This paradox of America was to be a major thrust of Russian—and indeed more recent Soviet—views of Americans. On the one hand, America stood for models of political organization and technological diffusion that Russia should emulate; on the other, it represented practices to be avoided.

American technology was closely observed by Russians, particularly as it might apply to the Russian economy. Although the technology of America was important in transportation—Nicholas I sent engineers in 1839 to look at railroad construction, and in 1853 naval officer A. S. Gorkevenko published a report in *Morskoi sbornik* about the clipper ships in Boston—it was really in agricultural production that the United States was most interesting.

AUTHOR'S NOTE: The author thanks the John and Mary R. Markle Foundation for its support of the larger research project, of which this is part.

This is particularly important, because it was precisely in agriculture that America challenged Russia's long-standing dominance of the international grain trade. Here was surely a profound reason why the two countries should be enemies, yet in spite of this natural competition, Russia saw the practicality of looking at America not only as a competitor, but also for the useful exchange of information. Although it is true that there was specific interest in tractors and grain elevators, there was also something else that caught the Russians' attention. Writer and traveler Evgeny Markov wrote in *Russkaia rech* in 1881 that Americans succeeded because they relied on individual initiative. He even went so far as to recommend that Russian agriculture follow the example by removing the heavy hand of bureaucracy: "Without any vice-governors and officials on special assignment the Russian people will comprehend its own agricultural needs, which have long been well known to it" (*Russia Looks at America, 1988, p. 129*).

Many Russian observers looking for models in American technology also found political examples of great interest. For example, the Russian diplomat Pavel Svinin wrote in 1814 about an innovation he called the *Stimbot* (steamboat) and praised America's talent for technological adaptation. But he was also impressed by the enormous influence of the American press, the spirit of American philanthropy, and the role of public education. Yet at the same time he wrote "money is a deity for the American" and warned that more crime would surely follow, not to mention the corruption in government he had already observed (*Russia Looks at America, 1988, p. 16*).

From America's experiments in politics, different Russians came away with very different impressions. For some it was the spirit of American utopianism in the nineteenth-century communes in America that excited them. These were the experiments that Robert Owen introduced, that Charles Fourier had imagined, and that religious communities had founded. A group from Kiev, including Vladimir Dobroliubov, the brother of the radical critic, and Vasily Alekseev, tutor of Leo Tolstoi's children, lived in American communes in the Middle West. And one should note the Mormons and the Shakers, whose communal life-styles fascinated Russian visitors depressed by the growing influence of corruption and the destruction of small economic enterprises in their native country.

During the period before the revolution he was to lead, Vladimir Lenin too turned to America. He was profoundly interested in the field of industrial management, particularly the work of Frederick Winslow Taylor, and also in the operation of the New York Public Library which, with its 42 branches, made books available to all classes of the population, as Lenin wrote in 1913 in *Rabochaia pravda*.

But America's experience struck Eduard Stoeckl, envoy of Aleksandr II, as dangerous. The elections, he said, incessantly repeat themselves and always give rise to scenes of disorder and anarchy. The famous scientist Dmitri Mendeleev during his 1876 visit announced that America had appropriated "not the best, but 'the mediocre and worst aspects of European civilization'" (*Russia Looks at America,* 1988, p. 185).

It is interesting to note that even under conditions of demanding economic competition, relations could be conducted cooperatively and the best models could be brought home. Sergei Kareisha, who wrote a book on American railroads in 1896, said that his work was *helped* by the very fact that he was a Russian and that the majority of Americans were favorably inclined to him. In his book he thanked the more than 40 American governmental agencies and rail firms that helped him.

Although at the end of the 1870s many German publications warned of American competition, calling it the "American peril," this was not true of most Russian responses. A. S. Ermolov, minister of state property and agriculture, gave a toast in 1894: "In the future there may arise in this area [industry] competition and even a clash, but an honorable and useful one, not destructive but capable, rather, of strengthening the organisms of state" (*Russia Looks at America,* 1988, p. 214). This approach, I believe, had great significance for the years ahead.

I would also draw one more general conclusion from this summary: The many varied political and economic aspects of American life were seen as just that. Some parts of American life, such as elections, the press, the educational system, and individual economic activity, were attractive for their democratic extension of popular control. Other aspects were seen as corrupt, exploitative, or just plain vulgar. They all coexisted and there is little doubt that Russians knew more about America at that time than most Americans knew about Russia.

Today some of this long historical record seems very fresh. There is still an asymmetry in what Americans and Soviets know about each other. Soviet mass media still pay much more attention to the United States than vice versa, although in the recent past that distance has narrowed substantially. America is still of the greatest importance to Soviet media, particularly television, in many of the same ways that it was so many years ago.

Comparative Soviet and American Television Project

There can be no doubt as to the influence of television as a powerful educator and socializer in Soviet and American societies. Recent studies have pointed to the effect of television on what kinds of issues Americans consider important and even on how they evaluate their leaders (see, for example, Shanto Iyengar and Donald R. Kinder, *News That Matters: Television and American Opinion,* University of Chicago Press, Chicago, 1987). Other studies have shown that the role of anchors and experts on the American news is key to the public agenda (see Benjamin I. Page, Robert Y. Shapiro, and Glenn R. Dempsey, "What Moves Public Opinion," *American Political Science Review,* 81:23-43, 1987).

Some of these effects are already being seen or will surely be seen soon with respect to Soviet television. Television in the Soviet Union, too, has become the principal source of news and information for the majority of citizens and viewing time is increasing as well. In the Soviet Union children are reported to watch television for up to five hours a day, a rate that exactly matches that of American children. A Soviet observer noted recently that reading among youth had declined significantly. In his words:

> The mass media—radio and television—have become much more interesting and competent. They took time which before was traditionally devoted by the family to reading. . . . In the last 20 years the time adolescents spend on reading books has been cut in half. From 4 to 11 percent of schoolchildren practically don't read at all. ("Kniga i politika," *Argumenty i fakty,* No. 23, June 10-16, 1989, p. 5)

The process is interactive. An increasingly attentive public of all ages is seeing television programming used much more cannily by a more savvy and capable political leadership—a leadership that is developing a relationship with viewers. Prime Minister Nikolai Ryzhkov's trip to Armenia after the earthquake was heavily covered by the Soviet news and resulted in a much more positive identification with this leader. He became a "personalized" leader. The election process depended heavily on the personalization of the candidates, and this was effected largely by television. Boris Yeltsin, Nikolai Shmelyov, and other noted candidates credit television with their victories. Conversely, those party and government functionaries who cannot operate in the relatively loose atmosphere of television and respond convincingly in a debate or question-and-answer situation will be disadvantaged. In short, those who cannot appear to be responsive and effective to the viewing public will, under the new system, be increasingly sidelined. The age of television politics has arrived in the Soviet Union.

Indeed, the coverage of the Congress of People's Deputies was so riveting that work stoppages and slowdowns occurred across the country during the broadcasts in the spring of 1989. There appeared to be little genuine competition for viewers' attention. According to Andrei Sakharov, even though the decision to televise the sessions at first met with resistance on the part of some in the party apparatus, the decision in favor of heavy live coverage produced an unprecedented event:

> This is an extraordinarily important thing, completely new in the history of the country. And considering the particular political character of our Congress,

completely new in world history. The televised debates attracted huge attention and served the further politicization of the population. A very great leap in politicization. I don't know whether or not this entered into Gorbachev's plans. ("Sezd ne mozhet sdelat vse srazu," *Literaturnaya gazeta,* June 21, 1989, p. 11)

In recognition of the increasingly central—indeed vital—role that television is playing the Soviet Union, we have been developing a program since 1984 at the Carter Center of Emory University to analyze Soviet television. We examine a range of variables: news flow, the representation of women, men, and minorities in news and entertainment programs, and issues of international security and arms control. For news programs, we have a computerized data base into which we have put coded analyses of each news program in our sample. (For a study of Soviet television and comparative analysis of Soviet and American television news, see Ellen Mickiewicz, *Split Signals: Television and Politics in the Soviet Union,* Oxford University Press, New York, 1988. For a study of the representation of ethnic groups on Soviet television news, see Ellen Mickiewicz and Dawn Plumb Jamison, "Dilemmas of Diversity: Minorities and Television News," *Journal of Communication,* 1991.)

Soviet television has a strong international component. American network news, on the whole, devotes a considerably smaller proportion of its newscasts to stories with an international or foreign focus. A 10-year study found that the percentage of international stories in American network news averaged just under 40 percent (James F. Larson, *Television's Window on the World: Coverage of the U.S. Networks,* Ablex, Norwood, NJ, 1984). Before and during presidential elections, a domestic focus is especially evident: A week in August 1988 yielded in our analysis only 26 percent international stories. During a later week, in February 1989, the proportion of international stories moved up to about a third of the total number of stories.

On the Soviet news, 66 percent of all news stories may be classified as international, that is, concerning some country other than the Soviet Union (perhaps, though not necessarily, in addition to the Soviet Union). This figure—66 percent—is *exactly* the same for six months sampled from three years: three months in the fall of 1984, two in the fall of 1985, and one in 1988. In general, for the allocation of time, though it is by no means identical to the allocation of numbers of stories (and in fact differs from it), the relationship generally is not reversed. A clear-cut exception was coverage preceding and during the Congress of People's Deputies and the Supreme Soviet in 1989, when individual stories about the sessions were extremely long. I will return to the question of elapsed time later.

From 1984 through 1989 the United States was the most important foreign country for the Soviet news. Fully 9.1 percent of all stories in the August 1988 sample month were stories mainly about America. This figure represents a substantial increase from the 7.5 percent recorded in the fall of 1985 (early in the Gorbachev period), which was itself a marked increase over the Chernenko period (fall 1984) figure of 6 percent. The United States in the August 1988 month-long sample claimed fully 14 percent of all *international* stories. Poland, which was third during this period, received only 6 percent.

The United States is becoming even more central than it has been before and the amount of news coverage reflects this increase. There is no question that in terms of images and models, the United States is in a class by itself, and its importance to the Soviet Union cannot be overemphasized.

Elapsed Time

Looking at the Soviet news in terms of elapsed time is another important dimension of analysis. Up to this point, we have focused on the percentage of stories. Here we will look at percentage of total time. Earlier research indicated that domestic stories (those that treated only the Soviet Union and no other country) had fallen from 36 percent of total news time in the Chernenko period to 30 percent the next year. Our August 1988 month-long sample reversed this trend with a very significant upsurge in time devoted to the Soviet Union—some 46 percent of total news time. Thus, although exactly the same ratio has been maintained over time in total number of stories, the weight of time has changed very impressively. This makes the centrality of the United States in Soviet news even more substantial: As time for other countries is declining, that devoted to the United States has actually risen.

"Vremya" allocated 6.1 percent of its total time during the month of August 1988 to stories in which the United States played a part. During the five months of our earlier study in 1984 and 1985, that figure was only 5 percent. If we take the elapsed time of stories in which the United States figured as a percentage of *international* stories, then the figure is 11 percent of total elapsed time of international stories.

No other country matches this block of time. The closest is Afghanistan, with nearly five percent of international news time, and Poland, with virtually the same weight. Eighteen other countries are given at least one percent of total international news time.

Newsmakers

We also coded for people who appear on the Soviet news. To be counted, the newsmaker would have to be identified by name, either in written or spoken form, whether or not he or she appeared on screen. In addition, those people who spoke on screen also were coded, whether or not they were identified. We did not include people who were shown but did not speak and were not identified. We coded for up to four people in a news story.

One of the most interesting findings of past research related to the leaders of the superpowers. During the three months of the Chernenko period we coded earlier, we found that the Soviet general secretary accounted for 8.5 percent of the newsmakers. That figure significantly increased in the fall of 1985, when the new general secretary accounted for 12 percent of all newsmakers. During August 1988, however, when Gorbachev was reported to have been on vacation, the figure plummeted, and he accounted for only 2.6 percent of all newsmakers whose citizenship and occupation were known (858 cases). It should be recalled that our coding scheme allowed us to count as newsmakers those individuals who were referred to but not shown. Therefore, even if Gorbachev was on vacation for some of that period and could not be shown, his name could still have been invoked in a variety of situations and he would still have turned up a newsmaker. This did not happen.

The American president accounted for 2 percent of all newsmakers in the Chernenko period; that figure rose substantially to 3.3 percent in the fall of 1985 under Gorbachev. However, mentions of President Reagan also declined to only 1.5 percent of newsmakers in August 1988. It is likely that Reagan's retreat to the background during George Bush's campaign and his wish not to upstage Bush at the Republican convention accounted for the drop.

In the 1988 sample Soviet citizens make up the majority of newsmakers, with 54.4 percent. The next largest category—and it is a very large one—is made up of Americans, who were 11.4 percent of all newsmakers whose citizenship was known. Only five other countries contributed newsmakers in excess of one percent: Afghanistan, Poland, Pakistan, India, and Rumania. Altogether, these five countries' newsmakers combined just about equal the American presence.

Affect

How polemical are Soviet news broadcasts as they relate to the United States? We were particularly interested in the use of clearly disputatious words. Do Soviet newsreaders or correspondents make judgments and evaluations about other countries?

In our earlier work in the five-month period we found that with respect to a characterization of a country as a whole by the official broadcaster or the correspondents employed by the State Committee for Television and Radio Broadcasting (Gosteleradio), approximately 17 percent of all international stories had a heavy overload of emotion. In the 1988 month's sample (August), a remarkable reduction had occurred: Only 6 percent of all international stories contained emotional rhetoric. The move to more neutral broadcasting had occurred. The practice of emotionally tinged or opinionated newswriting—the frequent and belabored use of such words as "criminal regime" or "racist government" or other traditional epithets—had declined dramatically. It was not entirely absent, but the environment of news writing had shifted toward more objective and neutral standards that we find in many Western broadcasts.

Non-News Programs

The news is not the whole of television but it is enormously important. We also looked at how the United States was portrayed in a number of television programs broadcast on "First Program" between September 1986 and October 1988. Some of these programs, such as the many spacebridges—live, interactive teleconferences—have been the subject of ample discussion, and I shall not add to it here. Suffice it to say that they were certainly pioneering and important events in international broadcasting and mutual understanding.

In other programming the record was less clear in the past. Certainly the way that the United States is portrayed has changed. And that is important, in my view, given that some of the programs we have analyzed were examples of very dubious television practices. For example, one film that played in prime time was the documentary *Babi Yar.* Made by Vitaly Korotich in 1981 but aired on television five years later with an introduction by Korotich himself for the 1986 broadcast, it is a brutal and graphic condemnation of the United States as the inheritor of Nazism. It mixes movie with news film, implying that both are equally factual, and is an example of an offensive departure from standards of moviemaking. Even as late as March 1988, the movie *Predosterezhdenie (Warning)* was another heavily polemical and emotional dramatization of half-truths about political and military subversion. Once again the United States was painted with the dark colors of base villainy.

A different kind of subversion was seen in several programs in this period that saw the spread of American culture around the world as the front line of the extension of American power (*Kamera smotrit v mir,* October 30, 1986; "What Does Mass Culture of West Serve?" April 21, 1987). I do think there *are* serious issues here and that they could and should be explored in a serious fashion. But these programs did not do so; they remained superficial and relied on polemical slogans, not empirical analysis.

Over the course of glasnost, in the climate of increasing cooperation, the depictions of the United States changed markedly. Some of the earliest examples of the use of America as a model were Vladimir Dunaev's pioneering story on McDonald's for "Mezhdunarodnaya panorama" ("International Panorama") and Carol Burnett's film on measures to treat alcoholism ("Beatrice—Life of the Party"). Here we see an objective look at American attempts to solve problems that are part of every nation's experience. Soviet television looked at American farm practices, computers, and the highway and telephone systems. These examples are reminiscent of earlier times when Lenin and those before him sought to adapt models from the experience of other cultures.

Clearly, to some degree the broadcasting of violently anti-American programming in the early part of this period was related to a wave of anti-Soviet movies and television programs in the United States, such as "Amerika" and *Rambo*. The negative programming on Soviet television came from an earlier Soviet past, a redefinition of which is also a very important part of the current stage of perestroika and glasnost.

In an edition of "Rezonans" in the spring of 1989, one of the participants referred to the American "opponents." He quickly corrected himself and said "partners." Other Soviet journalists have asked if acknowledgment of problems in the West is now considered "anti-perestroika." Certainly since the conclusion of the INF treaty and the reformulation of Soviet foreign policy by Mikhail Gorbachev, the television image of America has changed dramatically.

Conclusion

It seems to me that a new beginning has been made. The United States is exceptionally prominent on Soviet television news, an indicator of how important we are for each other. The dramatic reduction of emotionally tinged negative portrayals of the United States on the Soviet news and in documentary films—which take up a much larger proportion of total airtime on Soviet television than they do on American television networks—is very important for a future in which the huge television audiences in *both* countries will come to understand the other superpower. But some kind of new lens has to be developed in which the less positive features of our societies are as objectively treated as the more positive ones. And we have to deepen our analytic skills and become less superficial in our treatment of each other. Some will say that television is not the medium to perform this function in any society. With its rapid tempo and the assumed impatience of its audience (and the presumed inability or unwillingness of that audience to exercise highly developed cognitive skills), television lacks the capacity to probe these new relations fully.

An observer might also hold that Soviet television has not yet developed the capacity to perform in this fashion. As long as Soviet television news retains a protocol character, it will be impossible to get at the real news, such as, for example, the turbulent events in China in 1989. Soviet television news, especially the authoritative 9:00 p.m. (Moscow time) edition of "Vremya," still functions in part as an official adjunct to state protocol. Therefore, it represents the view of the state concerning foreign events. The massacre of students in Beijing was woefully underreported. Some Eurovision footage was used, but as the events unfolded, official Chinese government handouts replaced real reporting, and there was virtually no voice of the Soviet news at all. As an extension of official protocol, "Vremya" was implicated in the painstakingly slow and careful reestablishment of Chinese-Soviet relations and inevitably had a stake in the successful outcome of the Gorbachev visit to Beijing. At a roundtable discussion aired on television after the events in China, a Soviet commentator said, in answer to a question from a viewer about the paucity of news, that the news would not meddle in the internal affairs of China and would not take a position on the events there.

But the fact remains that the wide latitude and contentiousness that increasingly mark the coverage of domestic events has not extended very much into the realm of international affairs. An article in *Moscow News* decried the failure of Soviet foreign policy to take a stand on what it considered to be morally reprehensible conduct on the part of foreign governments or groups. In particular, the article criticized as insufficient Soviet positions on China, Romania, the Rushdie affair, and Palestinian terrorism. Television as adjunct to policy, the article contended, bore a heavy responsibility (Alexei Izyumov and Andrei Kortunov, "Diplomacy and Morals in Perestroika," *Moscow News,* No. 32, August 13-20, 1989, p. 6).

The foregoing analysis indicates that the Manichean vision of the world is receding for those who design and disseminate images of America on Soviet television. And with the decline of that vision comes a turn to more neutral practices of news and documentary film production. There are still, to use the Soviet term, "blank spots" in news coverage; there are still arenas of investigation that are off-limits; there are still imbalances in portrayals; and there is dissension and backlash among elites and masses alike concerning the course of glasnost. But remarkable changes have occurred and in many ways what one sees of the United States through the powerful and pervasive medium of television calls to mind a sense of continuity with the past before the Cold War in which images of America were complex and mixed; where some examples could be emulated and others avoided; where competition in global affairs was understood as unavoidable, but where the terms could be regulated by statutes, good sense, and mutual interests.

3

The Image of Russians in American Media and The "New Epoch"

GEORGE GERBNER

"The world leaves one epoch of Cold War," said President Gorbachev at his joint press conference with President Bush in December 1989, "and enters another epoch." What will that epoch be? More specifically, how will the "new epoch" deal with the legacy of some 40 years of hostility and distortion that poisoned the international atmosphere and provided the justification for repression at home and hot wars abroad?

A long-standing "enemy image" has deep institutional sources and broad social consequences. It projects the fears of a system by dramatizing and exaggerating the dangers that seem to lurk around every corner. It works to unify its subjects and mobilizes them for action. Behind the shifts from "red menace" through wartime alliance to "evil empire" and back to "Gorby-mania" are pictures, attitudes, and suspicions deeply embedded in the minds of many generations. Before considering how U.S. Cold War imagery may color or constrain the new epoch, it may be useful to examine that legacy and its lingering shadow.

* * *

The media are prime suppliers of the pervasive images "that depict the Soviets as inhumane, vicious torturers who enjoy inflicting pain and murdering children," writes Brett Silverstein in his article "Enemy Images: The Psychology of U.S. Attitudes and Cognitions Regarding the Soviet Union" in the June 1989 issue of *American Psychologist*. His survey of studies shows that American children's information about Soviets comes mostly from the media, with parents and school trailing far behind as information sources. Frameworks of knowledge are established early in life, and they are self-reinforcing as well as difficult to change. Silverstein cites polls showing that one out of four college students consistently underestimates the number of Soviet casualties in World War II and thinks that the Soviets first invented the atomic bomb. Press imbalances feed cognitive distortions. For example, *The New York Times* was five times as likely to mention martial law in a Soviet ally, or write about Soviet dissidents, than to carry news of the same things in a country friendly to the United States.

With the market saturation of what Cable News Network's Ted Turner called "hate films" in the May 17-23, 1989 issue of *Variety*—films such as *Rambo* (in which Soviet soldiers torture Stallone) and *Invasion U.S.A.* (in which two agents with rocket launchers cheerfully destroy a suburban neighborhood at Christmastime), the miniseries "Amerika" and the film *Red Dawn* (chronicling other Soviet invasions), and the film *Hunt for Red October* (a tale of a Soviet submarine commander's defection to the U.S.), it is perhaps not too surprising that 28 percent of those responding to a *New York Times* survey in November 1985 believed that in World War II the Soviet Union fought *against* the United States.

Things may be changing with movies such as *Delta Force II* and *Red Heat* showing Soviet and American cops and commandos, respectively, teaming up against terror in Chicago and the Third World. But the change is not always for the better. A "post-Cold War" episode of the CBS series "The Equalizer" showed Soviet scientists infiltrating the Pentagon and using U.S. research funding (maybe that's why there is so little left for *our* research!) to develop a torture technique that turns Americans into murdering maniacs.

Escalation of the body count seems to be one way to get attention from a public punch-drunk on global mayhem. The "Rambo" character played by Sylvester Stallone in *First Blood,* released in 1985, rambled through Southeast Asia, leaving 62 "commie" corpses. In the 1988 release of *Rambo III,* Stallone visits Afghanistan, killing at least 106 communists—just about one dead "red" a minute.

*   *   *

The wholesaler of enemy images, as of all images, is television. Prime time dramatic entertainment provides by far the most pervasive, frequent, and vivid images of all foreign nationals. Most Americans have never met a Soviet citizen, but they have encountered a Russian (always called a Russian, not a Soviet), in often intimate detail, an average of at least once in every three weeks of prime time network dramatic television. Only British and German nationals appear more frequently as major characters. Most of the "Russians" are stock characters typecast in the type of formula dramas that have fed the imagination of many generations of Americans.

Our analysis of these images is based on the University of Pennsylvania's Annenberg School Cultural Indicators data bank of annual network samples and a script archive consisting of all television plays since 1976. These sources yielded a sample of 44 programs with 103 Russian characters.

* * *

A fairly stable cast of about 150 major characters a week dominates the world of network television drama. Nine out of 10 are Americans. Russians are a visible presence in U.S. television's view of the world. In some ways, they are similar to the rest of the world presented on U.S. television. Russian men outnumber women about three to one, and their game is a game of power. There are no children or old people among the Russians. On the whole, they commit a little more violence than Americans (if that is possible, as about half of all television characters commit some violence). The aggregate personality profile of the Russians is more violent, strong, and efficient but, predictably, less successful than the Americans.

Taking a closer look makes all this come into sharper focus. Nine out of 10 Russian male and all female characters fall into just five categories. The largest is that of KGB and other secret agents, security personnel, and spies. Forty-five percent of the men and 17 percent of the women are in that category. The second largest group for men (23 percent), and the largest group for women (42 percent), is that of defectors.

So about two-thirds of Russian men and nearly as many Russian women seen on American television play out the roles of hunter and hunted. This being American television, most of the hunters fail, and their prey escape to "freedom."

The remaining one-third of the Russian character sample is divided among diplomats (9 percent of the men, none of the women), ballet dancers (6 percent of the men and 12 percent of the women), sports figures (6 percent of the men and 20 percent of the women), and scientists (12 percent of the women, but, curiously, only 1 man).

* * *

The image of Russians throughout the 1970s and 1980s is largely frozen into a frigid Cold War formula that does double duty on the sex role front. Men are the masterful, though ultimately vanquished, agents of a police state. Women are more likely to be fleeing from it. Meeting attractive Americans of the opposite sex always leads to a love interest that agents of the state must try to thwart.

These agents of the Soviet state, 9 out of 10 of whom are men, are depicted as cold, ruthless, and machine-efficient. "They know everything," whispers a victim. They do not trust anybody, especially women. "She is too soft," says one of them, speaking of a female agent. "Full of humanitarianism. It's ridiculous!"

Most of the men try to head off or reclaim defectors and watch over ballet dancers and diplomats. Their cover is often that of social secretary, interpreter, or journalist. They also steal U.S. secrets, kidnap U.S. scientists, and hoodwink U.S. "dupes." Nothing can stop their deception, murder, and terror except bullets and the CIA.

The defectors comprise nearly half of the women and one out of every four men. They are mostly dancers, sports figures, and spouses or family members of other defectors. They live in dread of the KGB. Their pathetic but ultimately successful struggle provides most of the human interest in the formula-driven plot configurations.

Comic or any other relief is rare in the world of Russian characters. Most of the humor revolves around their fractured English, like "Take the loaf off your feet." The otherwise relentlessly stark ritual is relieved occasionally by an attempt at genuine fraternization, as among Soviet and U.S. athletes (until the KGB puts an end to that), a medical rescue, a Soviet diplomat befriending an American boy, and a debate over the merits of hamburgers versus "Leninburgers." Probably unintended humor comes from sporadic attempts to "humanize" the attractions of a free society, such as the virtues of hamburgers, Tootsie Rolls, and Kentucky Fried Chicken.

One episode shows fighting among Russians, Chinese, and U.S. geologists on an expedition that ultimately ends in cooperation. Another, perhaps prophetic, depicts Russians and Americans getting together to fight Third World "terrorists." But none reflects the wartime alliance, the period of détente, or perhaps as yet, the "new epoch" in U.S.-Soviet relations. Most of the depictions delve into the most repellent aspects and fantasies of Soviet society and our most frightening and self-serving relationships with it.

*   *   *

With the projection of massive American military power into the Middle East, the geopolitical structure of the new epoch is only dimly emergent. Its cultural underpinnings are equally murky. The reservoir filled with suspicion and malice for half a century can be replenished at will. More than likely it can be turned, with appropriate adaptations, to new uses.

If the Cold War turns into a new "holy alliance," as some of those who declare themselves its winners seem to hope, the superpowers can concentrate on securing their ever more precarious hold on the remaining privileges and shrinking resources of a world liberated from some bankrupt forms of domination but increasingly free and open to symbolic invasion. The floodgates are opening for the penetration of Russophobic (and all other) media violence "made in the USA." Even (or perhaps especially) the Soviets are not immune. *Rambo* was reported to be the hottest video on the Moscow black market. After the "liberation" of the film industry, *First Blood* was "cleaning up at the box office," reported *Variety* (October 15, 1990, p. 66). No doubt it will go on to "free" Soviet television, to be followed by the even bloodier remakes. "To hear the Russians tell it," *Variety* noted, "the Soviet film industry liberated itself into a state of total chaos. . . . Many of the Soviet films are modeled after Yank B-pics. . . . As many as 70 percent of the new crop are "commercial, cheap and bad."

Few countries are still willing or able to invest in a cultural policy that does not surrender the socialization of their children and the future of their language, culture, and society to "market forces." That drift is more likely to contribute to the resurgence of neofascism than to that of an open, humane, democratic "new epoch."

The issue is cultural policy, not just goodwill or wishful thinking. The Cold War has contaminated the cultural environment at least as much as its physical counterpart, the deadly strontium 90, damaged the atmosphere. As with atomic testing, an active international constituency is needed to press for a new policy. A cultural environmental movement dedicated to democratic and humanistic media reform must build such a constituency if we are to repair and replace the dark legacy of the Cold War with something deserving of the name "new epoch."

4

Soviet-American Television: The Crucial Years

SVETLANA G. KOLESNIK

The transition toward the new political thinking, the new international morality and psychology now becoming a part of Soviet-American relations, requires the participation of the Soviet and American mass media whose aim is to serve the average citizen. The role of television is especially vital because it is the most influential channel of information.

The difficulties of that aim are caused not only by political barriers but also by the need to overcome the ideological stereotypes, prejudices, and oversimplifications that divide the world into black and white. This division has existed in both peoples' consciousness and produces the strongly politicized "enemy image" for both nations. But in speaking about this mirror effect, we must note one important difference; the Soviet Union has never treated the United States as an "evil empire," or an absolute enemy. Even during the most hostile years, Soviet mass media attempted to cover positively the life of the democratic part of American society and the cultural and technical achievements of the country. From that point of view, 1987 and 1988 were very crucial years for American and Soviet television. Two different television systems with different broadcasting backgrounds began to cooperate in an attempt to overcome the negative images they had created of each other's country.

In June 1988 the well-known American television journalist John Chancellor, summing up the results of the Soviet-American summit in Moscow, announced: "It seems that the 'Cold War' is over and soon we will have a parade." Of course it is too early to celebrate a victory but some positive changes are obvious.

The history of Soviet-American relations has been marked by many ups and downs, but we now have a completely different situation. Television, which became a new and extremely powerful medium in both countries during the years of confrontation, was used for proclaiming the armistice.

Chancellor's report showed that the traditional logic of political thinking had been discarded by the leaders of both countries and it also signaled a change in perception of American society toward the Soviet Union. These first signs of change were the results of new trends in international relations. From the Soviet side, changes were attributable to an accelerating process of reevaluation and a partial diminution of America in the enemy image. Both Soviet and American television have played an active role in the changing perceptions of both nations.

From the beginning of its existence as a mass medium, television has been the most vital channel for the formation of public opinion in both countries. That is why television systems in the Soviet Union and the United States find themselves under the strongest pressure of traditional political thinking. Nevertheless, television recognized the necessity to reject the political inertia that had earlier roots in the enemy image. Spacebridges—live, interactive teleconferences—appeared in 1982 as a result of Soviet and American television's attempts to find a form of possible dialogue. The decision of the Soviets to participate in these contacts should not be underestimated, given that at that time the U.S. government was not participating in many joint cultural programs.

The first spacebridges were made by Gosteleradio (the Soviet radio and television monopoly financed and administered by the state) and by small American television companies and university centers that had no possibility of gaining a national audience. As a result, the spacebridges had a negligible influence on American society. But for Soviet society, the spacebridges, which were seen by every adult citizen, served as a catalyst for overcoming the ideological and psychological differences between "us" (Soviets) and "them" (Americans). For Soviet television, the spacebridges provided the opportunity to reevaluate some attributes of the enemy image that for American commercial television became obvious only in the 1988 coverage of President Reagan's state visit to Moscow.

The first Soviet-American television spacebridges featured people famous in the fields of science and culture, including cosmonauts. They touched upon such vital themes as preventing war and preserving peace, the future use of atomic energy, protecting the environment, and other serious issues.

In May 1985, when the anti-Soviet campaign in the United States was at its peak, Gosteleradio, with the University of California at San Diego and the Roosevelt Center for American Policy Studies, produced a spacebridge titled "Remembering War: A U.S.-Soviet Dialogue." This program showed not only unforgettable footage of American and Soviet brotherhood during World War II combat but for the first time, ordinary people as well as celebrities discussing their impressions and reminiscences that contradicted the enemy image. "Remembering War," a program of the highest professional standards, was transmitted by all-union Program I (as all spacebridges were) and was repeated on Program II. According to Gosteleradio agency's estimates, over 100 million people saw Program I—practically the whole adult population in the USSR. Unfortunately, there were no American audience estimates available.

Unquestionably, the United States had the image of an ally for the USSR during World War II. The spacebridge appealed to the comrade-in-arms war memory of Soviet viewers and injected new blood into that image. But as positive as that feeling was, there was disappointment connected with the next spacebridge with the United States, "Citizen's Summit," a program moderated by Phil Donahue and Vladimir Pozner that linked studio audiences in Seattle and Leningrad in December of 1985.

Soviet-American experience in spacebridges spans more than eight years, and it is obvious that viewer interest has waned. But the influence of spacebridges on Soviet society has yet to be studied sufficiently.

Television dialogue between Leningrad and Seattle was prepared by a group of experienced journalists who had participated in organizing TV contacts, but the results of that program were unexpected even for them. Members of the Soviet television crew were not psychologically prepared to grasp how much the thinking of the participants was determined by the enemy image Americans still retained of the Soviet Union. The Soviet crew described their first impression in one word: shock. Vladimir Mukusev, one of the spacebridge directors and now anchor of "The Outlook," a program that occupies first place in the ratings, described his impressions: "Everybody present in the Leningrad TV control room was left with one feeling at the end of the TV bridge with Seattle—that it had been a complete failure."

The fate of the spacebridge, produced on the basis of the Central TV Youth Program, was determined in a heated discussion at the Gosteleradio administration. Opposing views were expressed, but the voice of Vladimir Popov was decisive. Two years after this, Popov was appointed to a key position, deputy of the chairman in the Gosteleradio administration. A carefully edited program was broadcast as a result of that decision. The main goal of the editing was to tone down the most glaring contradictions. But the careful cutting could not make participants more open, could not support a dialogue, and could not prevent the use of traditional schemes and clichés. The *Los Angeles Herald-Examiner* wrote: "The enormous gulf between Americans and Soviets could not have been better illustrated."

In blaming the Soviet audience for the political inertia, we must note that the Soviet-made enemy image was identical to the opinions expressed by the American participants of the spacebridge. This attitude largely determined the style of the dialogue, which was conducted by the American side in an aggressive manner from a position of superiority. What mainly hampers the process of mutual understanding is the stable anti-Soviet perceptions deeply embedded in the American mind. In some cases these perceptions cause total blindness to the reality of Soviet life. The situation during the subsequent TV bridge between Leningrad and Boston ("Citizen's Summit II," June 22, 1986) was the most striking example of this blindness. An American woman who sincerely believed that life in the Soviet Union was hard and miserable said, "I see that many of you are sad and suppressed." In fact there were no fewer smiling faces in the Leningrad audience than in the Boston audience. The statement by the American participant evoked bewilderment among the Leningrad participants and clearly showed that they were completely misunderstood by the American audience.

The aggressive style of the Americans provoked deep irritation among the Soviet participants and then among the Soviet TV viewers. Many considered the Donahue-Pozner spacebridges as "an insult, a mockery of the country" (L. S. Danilova, Chelabinsk). "Phil Donahue, with 20 years of journalistic experience, doesn't seem to have realized where he is," wrote N. N. Nedilko of Ineprodzerlinsk. "They have plenty of their own faults while they try to find faults with others. I believe the Soviet press and I am terrified of the things I read about America. America is a mad house: crime, drugs, etc." This letter was only one of many received by Gosteleradio.

An incident typical at the beginning of the glasnost period is worth mentioning. Some members of the Gosteleradio staff began searching for quick solutions to overcome the difficulties connected with the Soviet participants' behavior. A proposal to organize special psychological treatment for the participants was discussed. It is more likely that two years earlier the idea to solve difficult problems resulting from the society's development would have been implemented by the use of some fast means. But in 1987, Soviet TV was in the process of rethinking its functions in the new circumstances of a society speeding toward democratization.

In the framework of Gosteleradio, there is a constant struggle between transferring the accent from interpretation to fact. In January 1990 the new Sunday information program "7 Days" premiered. A. Sagalaev emphasized that this particular program "would not strive for imposing its opinion on viewers but it would have an intention to show its position." Three weeks later the chairman of Gosteleradio, M. F. Nenasheve, declared at a press conference that "first of all, television's duty was to inform and then to persuade the viewers." When answering questions later, he was forced to recognize that the healthy balance between fact and its interpretations required by our society had not yet been achieved.

However, the necessity to change the attitudes toward TV program content has been understood by Gosteleradio since 1987, and it has promoted the transition to new forms of broadcasting. After taping a series of spacebridges with the United States and West and East European countries, Gosteleradio did not follow a part of Soviet society in being unable to overcome the emotional barrier that was borne by the natural resistance of people's consciousness to the flow of disturbing information. The main thing in this flow was the extraordinary difference between the earlier formed image of "ourselves" as the mirror reflection of the enemy image and the new vision projected in spacebridges.

The study of this particular reaction brings us to the conclusion that one of the most important results of the spacebridges was the opportunity for the Soviet TV participants to look at themselves more objectively and evaluate their attitudes of superiority and infallibility. Many realized that they were partially guilty in failing to maintain a dialogue with the American participants. In one sense the Soviet-American spacebridges portrayed Soviet society and, after looking at this portrait, Soviet people discovered that they disliked it. It was a very positive mood in which to start the perestroika process.

Without a doubt, one of the most important Soviet perceptual changes of American journalists came about as a result of the spacebridges. The Cold War experience promoted a mainly negative vision of the American journalist as a person without principles ready to do anything for money. The film and television industries were mostly responsible for that skewed image. But the image of the American journalist in Soviet media was sufficiently pluralistic. Sergei Gerasimov gave us one of the best examples in his famous film *Journalist,* where for the first time an American journalist was presented as an attractive and honest person. However, he was also a conformist, able to write the truth only on one side of his notebook; he devoted the other side to his editor's orders.

These were the viewers' attitudes before they saw for the first time an American TV program with an American as an anchor. It was Phil Donahue and his show "Donahue in Russia," a program that focused on many of the realities of Soviet life. This show was unusual for the Soviet public in its frank discussions of normally taboo subjects within Soviet culture. Gosteleradio received many angry letters from viewers who were offended by the program.

Phil Donahue was the first American television personality who had the opportunity to expose his vision of the Soviet Union to the Soviet TV audience. A large part of the audience was not ready to accept the official changes in attitudes towards the U.S. press and refused to admit Donahue's right to investigate the difficulties of everyday life in the Soviet Union. A program made by Phil Donahue about the Soviet family became a cause of strong indignation. More than 50 percent of the letters addressed to Gosteleradio in connection with "Donahue in Russia" were in reaction to that particular program. Critical responses made up 78 percent of the reaction. Many of these letters, which often used ideological stereotypes and political labels, treated Donahue as an enemy. "Deep in our hearts we were indignant because of a program made by the American journalist Phil Donahue about the Soviet family! This American can be understood, by this provocation he earns money, but you, television employees, you are Soviet people! Why was he allowed to offend us in our own country and you assisted him?" wrote the Ivanovs from Sevastopol. The letter sent by N. J. Pilshikova (Moscow) was even more sharp: "Stop following the political saboteurs! Let our commentator ask the Soviet audience."

Why did a program about the Soviet family cause such indignation? Five hours of "Donahue in Russia" touched upon such tough subjects as Chernobyl, Jewish emigration, the Soviet army, youth problems, and family relations. But analysis of the mail allows one to conclude that some viewers could not accept the freedom by which Phil Donahue (who they believed to be a representative of the United States—a country with low moral standards) attempted to study the sexual problem in Soviet society. The program opened the possibility for a new perspective on the subject of sex, which has been, despite its extreme importance for the common people, completely ignored by the Soviet press. Moreover, the majority of Soviet people tend to consider sex a traditional taboo topic in Russian culture.

"The program made me so shocked as if somebody spat on my face," S. P. Romanova wrote to the editors of Donahue's show called "The Family Circle." "Why was Phil Donahue allowed to speak freely about everyone's intimate life for the whole country? Here in Russia we have never approved of that," wrote women factory workers from Sverdlosk. "It is blindness to hand a microphone to Phil Donahue," scolded N. P. Chennikov from Tagannog.

But besides these warnings it was obvious that because of the Donahue show, any new or different outlook on sex would be a closed issue for a long time. Or, more accurately, the spacebridge between Leningrad and Seattle influenced the Soviet audience's thoughts in this direction. The occasional comments of the participants reflected Soviet society's attitude towards that problem. One participant, a doctor, simply said, "We have no sex." From that moment only the rare article about sexual culture in our country managed to be published without that popular quotation.

It seemed that the under-45-year-old age group was the most impressed by the Donahue program about Soviet family life. Thirteen percent of the letters addressed to Gosteleradio were from people in this age group who expressed gratitude to Donahue personally for his program and rated his journalistic skills highly. V. Pasternak of Latvia in a letter representative of the younger Soviet audience characterized Donahue as a journalist having "the brilliant ability to improvise with wide erudition and intellectual freedom, as a person who can express his ideas sincerely with political courage." In contrast, among those over the age of 55 who wrote in, only 4 percent offered favorable comments.

The programs of 1987 made on the basis of Soviet-American cooperation set the stage for the undoing of the enemy image. Rapid democratization of the Soviet political system allowed the media considerable freedom in selecting and interpreting the different items. And this new mass media policy resulted in certain structural changes in television. Some new programs appeared, including "120 Minutes," "Before and After Midnight," "The Outlook," and some others that opened the channels of information about domestic and international events.

But besides this new process, the spacebridges as a form of television journalism were very popular. Gosteleradio estimated in 1987 that 70 percent of interviewed persons saw all the spacebridges broadcast in the USSR; 30 percent saw them from time to time, with people who preferred not to see that kind of Programing not included. Nevertheless, even in that productive period for the spacebridges, Gosteleradio began to devaluate them as a TV journalism format, using them mostly for internal Programing. Sometimes Gosteleradio did not use a spacebridge but produced a link by radio connecting two towns in the Soviet Union.

In spite of this, the Soviet-American spacebridges contributed to the improvement of the image system inculcated in the consciousness of both peoples in the period of the Cold War. A spacebridge series, "Capital-to-Capital," was produced by Gosteleradio in cooperation with ABC News, and for the first time in the history of spacebridges they were broadcast live and simultaneously for American and Soviet audiences. This series was extremely vital to the erosion of the enemy image. The "Capital-to-Capital" spacebridges gave the average American and Soviet citizen an exceptional opportunity to see political leaders at close range. And for the first time many Soviets got the chance to create their own image of American politicians, not on the basis of Soviet caricatures but by seeing their faces on the screen. The research department of Gosteleradio estimated that almost 24 percent of those who answered a questionnaire noted the "Capital-to-Capital" programs as the best programs of the year.

On the American side, the most interesting result was in the attitude changes, especially regarding the forms of TV dialogue possible with the Soviet side. The first spacebridge of the series made it obvious to the ABC News crew and the politicians who participated in or saw the program that an aggressive style in conducting TV dialogue with the Soviets was an unproductive one. As Elizabeth West, the producer of the spacebridge, said, "Americans must develop a new style in debating and must stop pressing the other side."

At the end of 1987 and beginning with Gorbachev's visit to Washington, Soviet television aired nationally a number of important programs that contributed to eradicating the enemy image from the Soviet audience's consciousness. The Soviet media coverage of the general secretary's visit became the next step on that road, a rare opportunity to show the state visit against the broad background of American life. But Gosteleradio did not take full advantage of this opportunity for several reasons, some of which were connected with the financial and technical level of Soviet television. Gosteleradio also did not veer from a pattern developed earlier, which was intended to concentrate its resources on the coverage of key political figures. Within the framework of that task, the Washington cultural environment was apparently considered less vital. The Gosteleradio programs broadcast from the United States were constructive and positive and provided excellent examples of de-escalational rhetoric in covering the official events, but the coverage of Washington life was fragmentary and in some parts was based on the old schemes.

At the same time, the three American networks, trying to probe Moscow's reaction to the events of the Washington summit, showed the mosaic of Soviet life. They filmed the empty shops and the discontented housewives but also tried to show examples of the new "Russian vision" of U.S. policy. "The blue bears of perestroika are sold in Moscow" was the summary of the CBS reportage from a toy store. Despite the sharp criticism of Soviet reality, this attempt to change the image of the Soviet Union as a "monster bear" was the main success of the networks' broadcasts from Moscow. In December 1987, Gorbachev, through his outstanding personality, had changed the average American's stereotype of Soviet politicians. At the same time the networks' bureaus created the foundation of a new attitude in U.S. press coverage of domestic life in the USSR.

The coverage of the Moscow summit in May and June 1988 gave even more impressive examples of the ways in which the American networks were trying to cast aside the absolutist and ideological forms of covering Soviet life. For the first time in Soviet-American history, the American mass media were officially permitted to cover all subjects they were interested in, from the military academy to the Moscow patriarchy residence. And the American journalists in Moscow were able to offer a colorful and multifaceted portrait of Soviet reality. The opinions of different layers of Soviet society were presented in those programs: Workers, flower sellers, people working in the state and party apparatus, militiamen, members of the government, and many others answered the questions of the American correspondents. Although some coverage was marked by a pursuit of Soviet exotica, the coverage on the whole was seen as an attempt to understand the different types of life in the USSR—based, of course, on the journalists' own perceptions.

Nevertheless, American journalists have rejected only the most crude stereotypes of the Cold War era and are still using their polished versions. An analysis of the networks' Programing from Moscow during President Reagan's visit gives us many examples. All the networks regularly showed Soviet women with brooms or shovels. Sometimes Soviet women were filmed while preparing the road for the asphalt works. The soldiers marching near the Kremlin wall became another popular video image. All of these images are a part of Soviet reality and they are truthful, but the networks' repeated use of them in virtually every airing distorted reality.

Today on network television it is difficult to find a portrait of the Soviet Union as a wicked bear, but this image does still appear from time to time. Broadcasting from Finland, the NBC anchor asked how the Finns were doing when "the Soviet bear is behind the next door."

Astonishingly, murmurs of the Cold War can be heard in Moscow in commentaries of the American news bureaus, whose journalists are so close to the object of interest. The networks' journalistic staff in Moscow as a rule don't have enough knowledge of Russian history and culture and generally don't speak Russian; therefore, they are forced to work within a so-called electronic cocoon. Under these circumstances they are trying to lean on familiar ideas and, as a result, they are painting a complex and multicolored Soviet Union with only a few colors of the palette. In the spirit of the Cold War the networks' Moscow bureaus are also still portraying the USSR as a militaristic superpower. Regardless of the subject, they consistently focus on nearby military service personnel. As an example, after watching the coverage of a rock concert one might get the impression that only military men and soldiers enjoyed rock music. This pervasive effort to pick out military personnel in every crowd, on every street, during people's holidays and sporting events, smacks of the Cold War days.

Moreover, American journalists are turning from the conception of "Soviet militarism" to the idea of "Russian militarism." The CBS correspondent Tom Fenton, discussing the growth of self-consciousness in the Baltic republics, illustrated the "Russian presence" via shots of soldiers. The detailed analysis shows that now many negative features of "Soviets" are connected with the notion of "Russians." In the same segment, Fenton affirmed that only Russian factories could be blamed for the pollution of the Baltic republic's environment. Although this problem ranks very high in the USSR, he linked the defects of mass building construction mainly with newcomers from Russia. Fenton's coverage exemplifies the attitudes and ensuing news coverage of American journalists working in Moscow.

In analyzing the activity of Soviet and American network television, we come to the conclusion that during the last two years both TV systems have made very positive moves in eliminating the enemy image. Of course this work has been possible only within the framework of developing political contacts between the two countries. Gosteleradio and American television giants have come to the mutual understanding that it is in both countries' best interest to cover each other truthfully, without using misleading stereotypes. This optimistic shift toward a more correct portrayal of one another is a very complicated and contrary process. The process, apart from some symptomatic successes, is obviously not in its final stages.

5

Images of the Soviet Union in the United States: Some Impressions and an Agenda for Research

EVERETTE E. DENNIS

It is hard to imagine citizens of any country who are not vitally interested in how their country is portrayed elsewhere in the world. Thus it is especially noteworthy at a time when commentators are proclaiming the end of the Cold War that Soviet images of the United States, and American images of the Soviet Union, should be the concern of an international conference.

Given that media portrayals are thought to be closely linked to public opinion and public policy, they are especially important during transitional periods when people are most open to change. It is easy to speak glibly about mutual images and to describe them impressionistically without measurement or systematic assessment. All of us know that for each of the two great superpowers the image of the other is shifting, yet we rarely consider the multifaceted nature of the resulting images and what impact, if any, they have on people in the two countries.

Images or representations of people, ideas, and even nations have been part of the literature of media studies for decades. However, it is fragmented research typically reporting what the manifest content of a given medium has said about a particular topic. In the 1980s, as the beginnings of the end of the Cold War were reported in world media, scholars began to study such topics as the image of the Soviet Union in U.S. television entertainment programs, the nature and shape of news reports on television in the two countries, and such specific topics as comparative summit coverage. The result, as a June-July 1989 Moscow State University conference has reported, is a clearer and better understanding of media images in the two countries. Some of this emerging research is also concerned with the definition of news in the two countries, the changing nature of journalism, structural control of the media, government regulation, freedom of expression, and other issues. It is generally acknowledged that the Soviet media are changing faster than media institutions in the United States, especially with the introduction and convergence of the concepts of glasnost and perestroika. As important as the Gorbachev years have been to opening a new era of diplomatic relations between the two countries, the images we have of each other go back a long way, and their residual imprints on individuals and national psyches are part of our institutional memories.

Here I wish to consider several aspects of the news media and their functions in society, which are essential to any discussion of mutual images. I will also suggest topics and trends that might be explored by scholars and professionals who want to understand and better track the American view of the Soviet Union. Finally, I will link these considerations of content to what we know about the impact, influences, and effect of media on people, institutions, and society. After all, the images we see on television and in the print press almost always influence thought, sometimes shape attitudes, and occasionally determine behavior.

The task of connecting content concerns with media effects is especially pertinent at a time when scholars speak of a so-called paradigm shift wherein the "power" of the press is being reconsidered. Whereas once it was thought that media had direct and profound effects, later researchers doubted this and downplayed such influence. Since the late 1970s, however, students of the media have joined in what sometimes is called a "return" to a powerful (though qualified) effects theory.

Because media scholars often have an elitist penchant for serious images emerging from information and news, they pay less than full attention to the other functions of mass communication and the various media that fulfill them. Students of Soviet images in the United States are more likely to direct their attention to major elite newspapers, the television networks, prime-time programming, and on occasion the movies. Most comparative study involves the news and information functions of the mass media; images on the pages of major national and regional newspapers and on network news and wire services are likely targets for investigation.

Fortunately, this narrow band is expanding as critics and commentators probe all media functions and media organizations. There are news and information "services" provided by so-called tabloid television programs like "A Current Affair," "The Reporters," and "Geraldo," which are watched by millions of people, not to mention the supermarket tabloids like the *National Enquirer* with their blotchy headlines and breathless exposés.

The information media in the United States also are expanding. There are thousands of general-circulation newspapers and mostly specialized magazines, as well as on-line data bases. There are house organs, church bulletins, special newsletters, MTV news programs, and news programs directed only at children or the elderly. The connection between the information function of the media, defined as "pure news," and the opinion function of the media is sometimes fragile. But editorial pages, op-ed columns, television talk shows, talk radio, and commentaries all contribute to opinion making. Added to news and opinion is the entertainment function of television. Images are built in serious drama, arts programming, situation comedies, sports, variety shows, and other television content, as well as through magazines and other media that entertain. Moreover, in a capitalist society, no one would seriously dismiss the role of advertising, which casts a long shadow in image creation.

In each of the four functional areas of mass communication—news, opinion, entertainment, and advertising—there are many different kinds of media with different purposes, and most of them offer consumers differing portrayals of the Soviet Union. On the same evening that Americans were moved by Tom Brokaw's historic interview with Mikhail Gorbachev, they also may have watched commercials that portrayed Soviets as buffoons and prime-time entertainment fare crawling with conniving KGB agents.

In still another arena there were lingering images of great Soviet athletes competing in international sports and Soviet dance companies touring the United States and displaying their art on public television. These are only a few of the flickering images of the Soviet Union in the United States.

Clearly any researcher considering images must be aware of how necessarily complex and multifaceted this inquiry must be. Similarly, if Soviet or U.S. citizens concerned with better relations between the two countries are put off by the wide range of U.S. media images, it is well to remember that the United States, although increasingly internationally minded, still erects barriers to easy international understanding. For much of our history we were essentially an isolationist country, having thrown off the yoke of Britain and decried "foreign entanglements." Indeed, this was the warning of George Washington in his farewell address. Add to this the unyielding mandate of the Monroe Doctrine of 1823, which "bars" foreign powers from the Americas, and the backdrop of mutual relations is more coherent. Until recently, rather than celebrate ethnic diversity in America, we were more likely to insist on "Americanization," assuming that anyone who would become a citizen should speak English and cherish traditions dating back to the American Revolution. Also, until recently, we've insisted on "language purity," which means "English only."

So great is our parochialism in the United States that international visitors are sometimes surprised, even astonished by it. "How can a country so well-known and admired around the world be so blind to others on this planet?" critics sometimes ask. I recall a French scholar visiting the United

States who expressed exasperation over the paucity of news from his native country in the *Minneapolis Tribune,* the paper in the town where he was staying. In a three-month period, he said, one story was published about France and that was a one-inch item on the decline of beret production! When he confronted the local newspaper editor, he was told, "We don't edit this paper for visiting Frenchmen."

Thus U.S. media filter news and information as well as create images of the rest of the world in a fashion that they believe will be responsive to their audiences' interests. Television viewers and newspaper readers are thought not to want encyclopedic coverage of France, the Soviet Union, or any other country unless such coverage is especially pertinent and salient to them.

This issue—what makes information, opinion, entertainment, and marketing images of interest locally—should be the topic of another inquiry. For most of the American media, it is thought that information and images from abroad often follow foreign policy or great world events. Although sometimes a scientific discovery, such as the discovery of King Tutankhamen's tomb in Egypt in 1922, can set off a wave of interest in a foreign country, for the most part what attracts attention and interest is international economic competition and armed conflict. The larger countries generally are covered most, as well as the places where we have cultural or sentimental attachments. The exotic and bizarre also attract the eye of the American media. Considerable and sustained interest in Japan and things Japanese is linked to a perceived economic threat. World trouble spots like the Middle East or Central America pose a national security threat and are thus of interest. In certain communities, links with the "old country," whether in Mexican Texas or California, Cuban Florida, Scandinavian Minnesota, Italian New York, or Irish Boston, foster fuller international images.

Because foreign policy is a major factor in our media images, cues about official American interests are useful in assessing international media coverage. Speaking in April 1989 (before the revolutions in Eastern Europe and the 1990-1991 gulf crisis) to the American Society of Newspaper Editors, Secretary of State James Baker sketched out foreign policy priorites for the United States. At the top of his list: the Soviet Union and China. Further down he mentioned the European alliance, the Middle East, Central America, and the Third World. A useful research project would be to track media attention to these areas and regions as the Bush administration's foreign policy evolves in search of a possible correlation between U.S. foreign policy and international news coverage.

I would argue that the image of the Soviet Union in the United States is best seen through the prism of media attention (across the several functional areas) to matters deemed either important or interesting. If I were fashioning a research agenda, I would urge students to consider tracking images through rigorous analysis of some of the following areas and topics:

Superpower competition. This includes national security coverage as well as economic considerations. At least since Lincoln Steffens' visit to Russia shortly after the Russian Revolution in 1917, when he declared, "I have seen the future and it works," attention has often been riveted on matters of competition. Nearly a half century later Nikita Khrushchev threatened to "bury" us economically. Closely linked to the general idea of national security and resultant "red scares" has been a general capitalism-versus-communism emphasis in our view of the rest of the world. Finally, what could have been a better metaphor for security, comparative ideologies, and national achievement than the space race that began in the 1950s and continues in a somewhat more cooperative vein today?

Soviet leaders. Americans have had particular images of Lenin, Stalin, the one-time team of Bulganin and Khrushchev, then Khrushchev himself, Brezhnev and his short-lived successors, and, finally, Gorbachev. The image of each of these leaders has been a personification of what we thought of the country at a given time. Most Soviet leaders have been seen as threatening and less than warm and responsive individuals. For a time during World War II, when the United States and the Soviet Union were allies, Joseph Stalin was affectionately called "Uncle Joe" by Franklin D. Roosevelt, but this quickly changed after the war and as the Cold War accelerated. During this period there was an issue of *Time* that featured "Our Soviet Ally" as the cover story. The general theme was that Soviets are "just like Americans" (both had overthrown monarchies, were informal and hardworking, governed by honest people, etc.). Although there have been fleetingly positive images of some Soviet leaders, it is my impression that their overall portrayal in the United States has been quite negative until Mikhail Gorbachev, who is seen as a bold reformer with a Western style. So popular has Gorbachev become in U.S. media, especially after the Washington summit of December 1987, that a *New York Times* editorial in 1989 declared that if an alien arrived on the planet and asked to be taken to "your leader" in most parts of the world, the Soviet president would qualify as the most visible and exciting leader in the world today.

Soviet history. Soviets may be surprised to learn that U.S. media have often been attentive to Russian history. True, we have overromanticized the Russian royal family in movies, television, plays, and books, but we have carried with us images of early Russian history, great figures from the royal court, and statecraft, as well as our own peculiar relations with the Soviet Union. In some instances the preoccupation with the Russian monarchy might be one way of contrasting the pre-Soviet period with what came after. Often the depictions of court life are gay and colorful whereas portrayals of the period after the revolution are grim and foreboding. In fact, American portrayals of both pre- and postrevolutionary Russians are caricatures that do little to enhance our understanding of life there. In addition, our purchase of Alaska, the role of the Russians in America, including California's Fort Ross and much more, has found its way into folklore and legend. Most of this treatment is quite positive, even romantic. Media attention to the Soviet Union was occasionally linked to the passage of espionage legislation in 1917 and 1918, as well as periods of deportations and "red scares," especially between 1917 and 1920 and 1948 to 1957 or so.

Foreign policy conflicts. Foreign policy matters have long dominated our view of the Soviet Union. This goes back to conflicts with the Japanese at the turn of the century, through two world wars and, more recently, in such places as Cuba, Afghanistan, Angola, and the Middle East. Here questions are always raised about motivations: We assume that the Soviets are up to "no good," meaning activity not in the best interests of the United States, and generally this gets bad press.

Soviet science and culture. Early on, American media portrayed Soviet scientists as unimaginative copycats, stealing U.S. secrets, especially the atom bomb, although the passing of secrets was less in the realm of science than espionage. More recently there has been admiration for Soviet achievement in space sciences and other fields. Soviet scientists, of course, also became well-known in the United States because of dissident activity. On the cultural front, Soviet ballet, chess, and other artistic and cultural achievements are much admired in the United States. From the Russian literary giants such as Pushkin, Chekhov, and Dostoevsky to composers like Tchaikovsky and Prokofiev and artists like Nureyev and Baryshnikov, this aspect of Soviet life has generally been warmly and enthusiastically portrayed in the United States through the several media, especially television.

Civil liberties. For several decades the concept of freedom—meaning individual autonomy from the state, or the lack of it—in the Soviet Union has dominated many American images of the USSR. From recent waves of immigration to Israel and the United States by Soviet Jews to the defections of dancers and KGB agents to the public protestations of the refuseniks, we have been bombarded by vivid images of people involved in a public dialogue over the meaning of freedom. More recently we have watched with fascination as that dialogue has heated up and gone public in the Soviet Union and elsewhere in the Eastern bloc. This is of fascination and concern to many Americans, and the media pick up the beat and theme.

Sports. Soviet sport has also lingered long as an image in U.S. media. At one time the dominant image of Soviet athletes was of hefty weight lifters and professional wrestlers. More recently, and especially since the beginning of televised Olympic coverage, a much fuller picture of Soviet sport has emerged. Runners, swimmers, gymnasts, basketball players, and others have emerged. Russian and other Soviet republic athletes are increasingly seen as physically talented and attractive. The brute image remains, though: Soviet athletes are often seen as cheaters, the "ones to beat," the "bad guys." There has also been considerable attention given to "biased" Soviet judges at the Olympics. Sports coverage of Soviets is wildly variable.

Soviet women. Soviet women have also held a fascination for U.S. media, mainly because of the range of roles they play in Soviet society. Images of female doctors, truck drivers, scientists, cosmonauts, spies, and other roles often dominated by males in the United States have intrigued American media consumers. Soviet women have enjoyed diverse images in U.S. media, from petite and elegant ballet dancers to essentially masculine (and ugly) sports competitors, engineers, and scientists. Americans have been perplexed by these images and often wonder about their accuracy and representativeness.

Peaks and valleys. U.S.-Soviet friendship has had its ups (1933-1939; 1941-1946; 1972-1978; 1986-present) and downs (every other year since 1917, the worst being 1917-1920; 1939-1940, when the USSR and Nazi Germany were allies; 1947-1957, the height of the Cold War; 1960-1962, the Cuban crisis and the Berlin Wall; 1968, the Czechoslovakia invasion; 1979-1985, the invasion of Afghanistan, and Poland's declaration of marital law, if fleeting images in U.S. media are any indication. From the days of John Reed, whose *Ten Days That Shook the World* was a best-seller in its day and later inspired Warren Beatty's epic movie *Reds,* to the touching story of the 13-year-old American schoolgirl Samantha Smith, Soviet-U.S. exchanges, from high school students to sports teams and dance companies, have been an important ingredient in any images we have of each other.

Unfortunately, the corpus of scholarship that tracks and traces images of our two countries in our respective media systems is quite limited. Some useful books and articles do exist and they add intellectual rigor to any discussion or debate of this subject. But the paucity of research suggests that much more is needed before any informed discussion of the image of the Soviet Union in the United States can be considered seriously.

The work fostered by the Moscow State University conference is an important start, as is the writing of distinguished American contributors like George Gerbner (on images of the Soviet Union in television entertainment programs), Ellen Mickiewicz (on television programming), and Daniel Hallin (on comparative coverage of summits). In the last two years there have been several doctoral dissertations and master's theses in the United States that take up these themes. Similarly, the work of the Center for War, Peace and the News Media at New York University has stimulated both student and faculty studies of news coverage. At three American universities that I know of—Columbia, Emory, and Michigan State—observers are tracking and studying Soviet television in joint ventures that bring specialists on Soviet affairs together with media scholars. Much of this work involves using such tools as content analysis, historical analysis, legal and regulatory study, and economic analysis. What will emerge, I believe, is a more cogent portrait of how the great superpowers see each other and themselves.

There is less attention to what this taking stock really tells us. Do these images reflect or help shape reality? Are they accurate and truthful portrayals, or misleading ones? And by whose standards? Do the mechanisms that "manufacture" news and create entertainment programs so deviate from the norm in the two societies that they obfuscate and obscure? More importantly, do they shape individual and institutional agendas? Do they influence thought and shape opinion? Do they, can they, influence behavior, both on a person-to-person level as well as between and among social institutions in the two societies and in their governments?

All of these are questions that beg answers. We do not yet have an accepted, comprehensive theory of communication and media effects that provides easy or discrete answers. What we do have is an informed body of literature and experience that offers clues. Media research has moved through several cycles since it evolved as a serious intellectual pursuit earlier in this century.

As scholars have indicated elsewhere, there was at first a rather simplistic view that media were all-powerful and could have profound and controlling effects on people and culture. Then there was a long period of serious reconsideration. Study after study failed to generate evidence to "prove" the power of the press's ability to change behavior or even change attitudes and opinions. Later scholars focused attention on cognitive effects, guided by Bernard Cohen's suggestion that the media don't tell people *what* to think but what to think *about*. These developments in the social sciences, which offer cautious approval for the idea that the media do have powerful effects, have been augmented by humanist scholars, historians, economists, and critical theorists who believe media under certain conditions to be quite powerful. This growing literature has not been applied to the Soviet-American image situation so far, but this ought to happen if the consequences of images are to be understood and appreciated.

What is the image of the Soviet Union in the United States? It is multifaceted and varies widely depending on what medium and what media function are being explored. The Soviet Union of the news columns and the editorial pages is not the Soviet Union of the comic strips, sports pages, or television sitcoms. The Soviet Union in opinion magazines is not the Soviet Union portrayed in commercial advertising. And so it goes. Essentially, though, our understanding of the image of the Soviet Union in our media is quite primitive (as is our understanding of other nations' images) and will benefit by the current wave of interest, which is sure to bring both substantive and methodological strength to an important research venture.

6
Images of Self and Others in American Television Coverage of the Reagan-Gorbachev Summits

DANIEL C. HALLIN

This chapter is based on research conducted jointly by myself and an Italian colleague, Paolo Mancini. Although I will focus on the American coverage, the study is actually a comparative one, dealing with television coverage of the Geneva, Washington, and Moscow summits on U.S., Italian, and Soviet television. In a way, the planning of our project gives good evidence of the extent of the changes in the Soviet Union and of the easing of the Cold War. At first we considered trying to find a Soviet scholar to work with us but concluded that the topic was too political for such a collaboration to work well. This book, of course, in part pursues exactly this kind of joint research. As it evolved, our summit study became very complex with many lines of argument—much too complex to summarize completely here.[1] Instead, I will offer a relatively simple discussion of dominant images of the Soviet Union in American television news and how they have changed in recent years.

The concept of *security* is a key concept of the nuclear age. Robert McNamara, the U.S. secretary of defense under Presidents Kennedy and Johnson, once expressed his view of security as follows: "Security depends upon assuming the worst plausible case, and having the ability to cope with it".[2] It is fair to say that this has been the predominant way of understanding security in both our countries since the end of World War II. We assume the worst of our adversary and prepare our respective military forces accordingly.

There are many problems with this policy, one of the most important being the cultural problem that is the subject of this book. The assumption we make about our adversary refuses to remain a mere thought experiment in which policymakers engage to be safe rather than sorry. It becomes part of a powerful image of the other, deeply rooted in our culture, which distorts our understanding both of the other and of ourselves. I believe this happens because for both of our countries, our own political identities have come to be defined in large part by opposition to our images of the other. These stereotypes have functions within each of our countries. Most importantly, they have become crucial to the way we construct our individual senses of self.

Let me take as an example here the American image of Soviet journalism. During the Reagan-Gorbachev summits there were many stories on American television about Soviet journalism. From Geneva, for example, ABC ran a story titled "How the Other Side Sees Things." The following are some excerpts:

> There is a tendency in the West to think that Soviet-bloc journalists are told exactly what they will write and say. Not quite. They don't have to be told the party line; they are part of it. . . . Soviet-bloc journalists, like their American counterparts, report on the comings and goings of Mr. Reagan and Mr. Gorbachev. Like American reporters, they go to briefings. And there the similarities end. It is the Soviet spokesman, Leonid Zamyatin, who sets the public tone in Geneva. It is the Communist Party of the Soviet Union, of which Mr. Zamyatin is a member, that sets Soviet journalism's policy. The willing-and-equal-partner approach this week is seen in the Soviet press as well. Last week, when the Kremlin was angry at the Reagan administration, the Soviet press was angry too. And what about the audience back in the Soviet bloc, when it wants diversity, another opinion? It listens to foreign radio, like the BBC or the Voice of America. ("ABC Evening News," November 19, 1985)

The real function of a story like this, I believe, is not so much to tell the audience something about Soviet journalism but to reaffirm the American journalists' image of themselves. And of course the most important part of that image is that they are politically autonomous, that they provide a source of information that is independent of the state.

Certainly there is much truth to this self-image. American journalists do have considerable autonomy from political control. We have seen an important example of this autonomy earlier this year, when the Bush administration was resisting new initiatives on ending the Cold War in Europe, and much of the American press was calling very strongly for "new thinking" on U.S.-Soviet relations. The independence that they exercised here is obviously no small matter coming in the highest and most sensitive area of political policy.

And yet this black-and-white image that says that our media are entirely different from their media, that we aren't influenced by changing state policies or by national prejudices, and that we just report the truth is very misleading.

A good example is a pair of stories by the same journalist—David Brinkley—from summits in two different political eras. Here is Brinkley at the Moscow summit in 1972:

> For twenty-five years the United States and the Soviet Union have spent *unbelievable* amounts of money, *mountains* of money, for weapons. Both countries have armed themselves against whatever threat existed, and whatever threat the most feverish and self-serving imaginations could invent. . . . If now at last the two countries have agreed not to stop but to start in the direction of stopping, one question might be, "What took them so long?" ("ABC Evening News," May 26, 1972)

Now here is Brinkley at Geneva in 1985, giving a history of great-power summitry: "Perhaps the first summit meeting was the Congress of Vienna in 1814," he began. "Even then, the Russians demanded control of Poland, and got it." The report then jumped to the beginning of the Cold War, and proceeded to give a history of U.S.-Soviet relations. Here are two excerpts:

> Potsdam, 1945. Truman quietly told Stalin the United States had invented a new, fearful kind of bomb. He did not suspect Stalin already knew it. His spies had already stolen the secrets of the atomic bomb, and delivered them to Russia.

> Vienna, 1961. Khrushchev, with the cold eyes of a Russian peasant, decided Kennedy was weak, tried to bully him . . . and . . . was fired for his bungling. ("ABC Evening News," November 15, 1985)

In the November 19 story, Peter Jennings described the Soviet media as changing with the political winds in Moscow; here we see that the American media also are affected by the political winds in their own capital, though certainly the processes of influence are different in important ways. The Moscow summit of 1972 came at the height of detente. The Geneva summit came at a time when the dominant tone in American politics was strongly anti-Soviet. The reason is complex and has to do with the ascendancy of the right in American politics. It also has to do with the war in Afghanistan, martial law in Poland, and other policies of the Brezhnev period. But it meant that at Geneva, American television had a strong emphasis on the traditional Cold War image of a hostile, aggressive Soviet Union. (This coexisted, certainly, with the hope that the summit would succeed and lead to an easing of tensions.) I won't elaborate on the ways the history of the U.S.-Soviet relations has been distorted by this kind of black-and-white image, but certainly Brinkley's history here was very one-sided and inaccurate.

Let me say a little more about why the Cold War tone of American television was particularly strong at Geneva, because it is a case that tells us much about the nature of the American media. Journalists who covered the summits of the 1970s have told me that the American side mostly dominated press relations. At Geneva it was different. Gorbachev and other Soviet officials were very active in courting the world media, though their efforts didn't always go smoothly. The game of international press relations is an unpredictable one. At some press conferences, for instance, critics of Soviet policies on emigration or political dissidence stole the spotlight. But in other ways this more active Soviet press relations effort was quite effective. It is interesting, for example, that Gorbachev actually appeared slightly more often than Reagan in the American coverage of Geneva. American television is, after all, looking for a good story, and Gorbachev was clearly a better story than Reagan. There is a very significant difference between U.S. and Soviet television; Reagan only appeared once in Soviet coverage of the Geneva summit, at the final joint press conference. No other American officials appeared at all.

But I think that American journalists, particularly television journalists, also reacted defensively to Gorbachev's more active public diplomacy. They feared that they would be accused of being manipulated by Gorbachev, and I think that is in part the reason that they made a special effort to reaffirm the old, familiar ideological commitments. It is important to stress here that journalists were worried about the *public* reaction even more than any reaction from government officials or owners of the media. After 40 years of the Cold War, images of the enemy are deeply rooted in the public consciousness, though again, they coexist with a strong desire for reconciliation.

In later summits, with U.S.-Soviet relations improving and Americans increasingly convinced that the changes in Soviet society were real and significant, the traditional stereotypes of the Soviet Union became less common, though certainly they did not disappear. The Soviet Union now plays a different role in confirming the American self-image. Before, Americans defined themselves in *contrast* to the Soviet Union. Today Americans more often see the Soviet Union as adopting and thus confirming American ideology. This is perhaps still a narcissistic view, and not always an accurate one, but it certainly leads to a much less hostile image. On the last day of the Moscow summit, for example, Charles Kuralt of CBS took a trip on the trans-Siberian railway. There he found two workers whom he used as symbols of the old and the new in the Soviet Union. One was a dining car waiter who loved his job because he didn't have to work; the other, a goulash peddler whose plucky hustle made him more money than a doctor. The waiter represented the old Soviet Union, and the goulash salesman the new. The two also represented socialist and capitalist man. Zhenya, the goulash salesman, in fact, was full of bourgeois wisdom. "As you guys say," Kuralt quotes him, "time is money." The story ended with Kuralt recounting how he had asked Zhenya how much he charged for the goulash—did he give it away?—to which Zhenya replied, "Oh no! I can't afford communism!" This story, incidentally, is as good an example as one can find of the highly mediated and populist style of American TV news. Far from merely summarizing the proceedings of the summit, American television goes out into the world in search of stories, preferably involving ordinary individuals with whom the audience can identify, that will permit the news to be placed in a larger ideological context.

In closing, I return to the concept of security. Real security clearly involves controlling not only the arms race, but also its cultural counterpart; it requires vast improvement in the quality of information our countries receive about one another, and the volume of exchange of ideas between us. There has, in fact, been great progress in this area in the last few years, and the exchanges between media scholars that we have recently initiated should play an important role of their own.

NOTES

1. Fuller discussions can be found in Daniel C. Hallin and Paolo Mancini, *Friendly Enemies: The Reagan-Gorbachev Summits on U.S., Italian and Soviet Television* (Provincia di Perugia, forthcoming) and "The Summit as Media Event: The Reagan-Gorbachev Meetings on U.S., Italian and Soviet Television" (paper presented at the 39th Annual Conference of the International Communication Association, San Francisco, May 28, 1988).

2. Quoted in McGeorge Bundy, *Danger and Survival: Choices About the Bomb in Its First Fifty Years* (Random House, New York, 1988), p. 544.

7

The Image of the United States in the Soviet Mass Media: The Results of Sociological Surveys

LARISSA FEDOTOVA

Practically all of our knowledge about images of the United States in the Soviet mass media is contained in journalistic articles and some political and cultural works. The empirical works on the theme are more rare and have come to light only over the last two decades. This can be explained by the fact that Soviet sociology was revised at the beginning of the 1960s.

The earliest attempts of empirical surveys on this subject took place in the years 1967-1969 with the Soviet Middle Town Public Opinion Survey conducted under the direction of Professor Boris A. Grushin. The investigation dealt with the information politics in our country both on the level of the information-making process and on the level of the state of mass consciousness as a receiver of that information.

The content analysis of Soviet Middle Town press showed that the amount of the communicators' attention to the capitalist countries was between one and six percent among the different sources. For the most part, the coverage focused on the capitalist countries as political systems. There were few instances of coverage of social issues such as those dealing with the economy, democracy, ideology, welfare of people, and opportunities for personal development. When these issues were covered they were mostly shown in a negative light. Indeed, 95 percent of the lean amount of social-issues coverage was negative.

It was no accident that the poll results showed dissatisfaction of the Middle Town people regarding social and economic information. When respondents were asked the question, "About what aspects of the United States would you like to have more information?" the topics eliciting the most interest were the life-styles and customs of the people (68 percent), the economy (64 percent), and issues concerning young people (55 percent).

60

In answer to the question, "What country would you like to visit most of all?" the United States was not as prevalent an answer as Czechoslovakia (66 percent) or France. Of the entire sample, only 43 percent answered the United States. The survey showed that the main sources of information about other countries at that time were Soviet newspapers and magazines (94 percent), Soviet radio (92 percent), and Soviet television (86 percent).

The Middle Town people evaluated American life with respect to the level of the development of the economy as 4.7 points (on a 5-point scale with 5 as the high end and 1 as the low end); the level of development of culture as 3.4 points; and the level of development of democracy as 2.3 points. The Soviet people evaluated their opportunities to equal the American life-style as follows: physical culture and leisure, 3.2 points; opportunities for prosperity, 3.0 points, and opportunities for education and profession, 2.8 points.

Regarding political characteristics of the United States, the overwhelming majority of Soviet respondents chose the following: "USA creates a situation of war tension" (99 percent) and "USA treats USSR with hostility" (81 percent).

More recent examples of information about the United States in the Soviet mass media can be found in content analysis studies of "Vremya" ("Time"), the main information television program of our country. These studies were conducted by the department of radio and television and some faculty in journalism at Moscow State University from 1984 to 1987. In the years examined, 7 percent of the total news of "Vremya" contained information about the United States. As shown in other studies, it was primarily political information: government activities, statements of political and public figures, statesmen, war activities, public manifestation, and so on. As a whole, capitalist countries, including the United States, were shown as political systems.

Tables 7.1 and 7.2 illustrate the prevalence of political information very eloquently. Moreover, the tendency takes place in dynamics—in 1987 as compared with 1984. Only the coverage of socialist countries and countries with a socialist orientation became more balanced. As for information about capitalist countries and the United States in particular, these disproportions also were seen as questionable by the audience.

A sociological poll of public opinion in Leningrad revealed clearly that the respondents felt there was a lack of information concerning the social aspects of American life. The answers to the question, "What aspects of American life must be covered, to your mind, more frequently in TV news?" are shown in Table 7.3.

Table 7.1
Subject Matters of News About Foreign Countries in "Vremya" in 1984

	Political	Social	Economic
Capitalist countries as a whole	76(24)*	18	6
United States	81(25)	19	0
Socialist countries	65(12)	26	9
Countries with socialist orientation	77(4)	15	8
Third World	80(4)	18	2

*in parentheses, the struggle for peace

Table 7.2
Subject Matters of News About Foreign Countries in "Vremya" in 1987

	Political	Social	Economic
Capitalist countries as a whole	71(5)*	25	4
United States	79(9)	19	2
Socialist countries	56(2)	16	28
Countries with socialist orientation	50(0)	43	7
Third World	82(3)	·15	3

*in parentheses, the struggle for peace

Table 7.3
Percentage of Leningrad Citizens Wanting to Know More About Aspects of
Life in the United States

The style of life, customs of people	66%
The life-style of different social groups	57%
The fine arts, literature	51%
The struggle for peace	46%
Leisure, entertainment	46%
Service sector	44%
Health and medicine	37%
Education	37%

Content analysis of TV news dealt with the statements about the role and position of the USSR and the United States and about the politics of peace and war. We used pairs of contrasting statements such as:

USA undertakes actions against disarmaments drive, withdraws the initiatives for peace/USSR struggles for peace and disarmament;

USA supports disarmaments drive/USSR undertakes actions on spreading armaments, ignores the peaceful initiatives; and

USA is for peace/USSR is against peace.

Table 7.4
The Authors of the Statement "USSR Struggles for Peace . . ."

Statements made by:	1987	1986	1984
Soviet representatives	49	44	72
Representatives of capitalist countries (other than United States)	28	30	10
Representatives of Third World	12	5	2
Representatives of socialist countries	9	5	13
Representatives of United States	0	15	2

Table 7.5
The Authors of the Statement "USA Supports Disarmaments Drive . . ."

Statements made by:	1987	1986	1984
Representatives of Third World	46	13	7
Soviet representatives	41	55	59
Representatives of capitalist countries (other than United States)	7	13	5
Representatives of socialist countries	3	10	14
Representatives of United States	3	3	8
Representatives of countries of socialist orientation	0	6	7

In none of the 1984 news stories did the idea that "USSR is against peace" appear. The idea that "USSR is for peace" appeared every day in two news stories, whereas the idea that "USA is for peace" appeared every second day in one news story. The idea that "USA is against peace" appeared every day in three news stories. Unfortunately, we only have the results for 1984.

Next we wanted to know some additional aspects of the arguments, in particular who the authors were. In other words, representatives of what countries made the statements that appeared in the "Vremya" news stories? The results are shown in Tables 7.4 and 7.5.

Concerning the authors of the statements about peaceful politics in the United States, all of them belonged to the Soviet correspondents because they were facts about peaceful demonstrations of American people.

Looking at the tables, one can see that the year 1986 looks more polyphonic, more balanced. The dramatic events in the last few years have significantly changed the whole political world and Soviet-American relations in particular. These events have also influenced Soviet and American public opinion and the content of both media systems. In this regard, it is important to mention the spacebridges between the USSR and the United States through which the peoples of the two countries got the chance to communicate directly, to look into each other's faces. The Soviet audience appreciated this unique opportunity to interact personally with American citizens. Responses in the press were full of statements such as: "I saw it myself, that . . .", "I had a feeling . . .", and "I disagreed with the view of theirs that . . .". The audience's newly acquired experience was far different from the picture of the world that had been formed by its own mass media.

Clearly, the more the public opposes the mass media's perception of the other country based on personal experience, the more the mass media will be obliged to reflect the life of the other country more fully and accurately.

8
Images of the Soviet Union in American Newspapers: A Content Analysis of Three Newspapers

WON HO CHANG

Historically, no international relationship has been more crucial to the survival of humankind than the twentieth-century relationship between the United States and the Soviet Union. These countries are accustomed to being adversaries. They compete for power, access to resources, and influence around the globe from Poland to Nicaragua and from the Philippines to Afghanistan, and the enemy image has been dominant in the relationship between these two super-nations. Since the beginning of the 1980s, however, the relationship between the United States and the Soviet Union has changed from one of adversaries to one of cooperators sharing dreams of peace and fears of war.

There is little doubt that the American news media's attitude toward the Soviet Union influences their interpretation of Soviet objectives. The media's assessment also influences U.S. policy toward the Soviet Union as well as the American public's perception and opinion of the USSR. Reporters, like the leaders of their countries, have seen the world in Cold War terms. It is rare to see accurate, sensitive reports by Americans on the Soviet Union, just as it is rare to see objective reports by the Soviets on the United States. Throughout history, mutual distrust has restricted the flow of information in both directions.

A decade ago the Soviet Union was called a secret society. But at the April 1985 plenum of the Soviet Communist Party, which elected Mikhail Gorbachev as president, the party proposed a whole range of ways to promote the democratization of Soviet society. Perestroika and glasnost then got under way. Today increased availability of direct information about the changes transpiring in the Soviet Union is perhaps the most important element in the erosion of the Western view of the Soviet Union as the enemy. The progress of perestroika, glasnost, and democratization appears to be changing people's attitudes toward the Soviet Union and the Soviet people.

The coverage of the Moscow summit in June 1988 was a big step for Mikhail Gorbachev's glasnost campaign. The American media, not knowing what was possible or impossible in this new era of vague definitions, simply experimented. They could employ glasnost both as a weapon and a shield: a weapon to push policemen aside and gain access to stories, and a shield to protect them from prosecution for their actions in the Soviet Union. There still are no definite boundaries of glasnost in the Soviet Union. Journalists in Moscow have to work in an environment where government restrictions and allowances are ambiguous and where they increasingly face choices about what is important for Americans to know.

As much as American reporters brighten the flame of glasnost, which in Russian means "light" in addition to its common definition of "openness," they also feed the kind of opposition that could darken Gorbachev's golden policy of "free flow of information." For Soviets who can barely tolerate glasnost, the free roaming of Western journalists has caused great consternation. The delicate dilemma Gorbachev faces in trying to integrate glasnost, a freer press, and political stability can be seen in the way the media covers Soviet dissidents. Whereas many Western journalists still gravitate toward covering the familiar scenes of contention as proof of the ultimate challenge to glasnost, more seasoned Moscow correspondents are beginning to listen to the crescendo of new and influential voices. In this context, the coverage of the Soviet Union by the American news media may influence Moscow's news coverage of itself.

Like other international news, coverage of the Soviet Union by American media depends largely on their own correspondents. The American correspondent Bernard Cohen envisions several roles for the journalist: as a neutral reporter, informant, interpreter, and visualizer of events; as an instant and continuous chronicler of transpiring events at crucial moments of intense national concern; and as a representative of people and an instrument of government. Critics of American coverage of the Soviet Union have long maintained that American correspondents tend to exaggerate the importance of dissidents.

Some observers, like Stephen F. Cohen, contend that the prevailing image of the Soviet Union in American media is that of a crisis-ridden, decaying system composed of a stagnant, inefficient economy; a corrupt, bureaucratic elite; a sick, cynical, and restive society; and an aging, inept political leadership that can't change or make policy, but only manipulate it.

Whether purposely or inadvertently, Cohen says, the American media err in three fundamental ways. The first is a focus on the negative side of Soviet life, ignoring such positive events as expanded welfare programs and rising living standards. The second is the use of language loaded wtih value and bias. And the third is that the press regularly assumes that the Soviet Union is guilty of every charge made against it. The unbalanced reporting to which Cohen refers stems from the old American media habit of assuming that the Soviet Union is wrong or guilty; the media's tendency to echo the prevailing tone of American politics, particularly as it emanates from the White House; the lack of information about the Soviet political system and culture; the lack of a professional corps of Sovietologists in the American media; and the laziness of correspondents with respect to learning about the Soviet Union.

Design and Method

The purpose of this study is to examine how three major American newspapers—*The New York Times,* the *Washington Post,* and the *Los Angeles Times*—portrayed the Soviet Union in the period from January 1988 to January 1989.

The method used for this study was content analysis. Three hundred articles were randomly selected from the three newspapers' front-page stories, editorials, and columns. The stories, except for editorials, were all over 10 column inches long. They were classified into 12 categories: political reform, economic reform, human rights, ethnic, military, government corruption, disaster, culture, business, diplomatic, social, and "other."

This study also measured attention scores for each story. The degree of attention was determined by six criteria: stories over 15 column inches, headlines over two columns, front-page stories, top stories, stories over five columns wide, and stories with a photo or illustration. Each of these criteria was assigned one point. The highest possible attention score was 6 and the lowest was 1.

The sources of the news items were also examined. They were divided into staff writers, wire services, contributors, and other sources. From this examination, we can learn the major sources of the three papers' news of the Soviet Union.

Favorable, neutral, and *unfavorable* are the three categories that measure the direction of the papers' reporting of the Soviet Union. The definition of these three categories is as follows:

Favorable coverage emphasizes international cooperation, a positive attitude toward Soviet reforms, social cohesion, political and economic stability, and moves toward democratic leadership.

Table 8.1. Direction of Reporting

Direction	New York Times	Washington Post	Los Angeles Times	Combined	Average
Favorable	35	37	28	100	33.3%
Neutral	48	46	34	128	42.7%
Unfavorable	17	17	38	72	24.0%
Total	100	100	100	300	100.0%

Unfavorable coverage emphasizes social conflicts, disorganization, political and economic instability, international tension, and a negative attitude toward Soviet reforms.

Neutral coverage is content that is balanced or betrays no controversial intention.

Analysis and Findings

Overview

The major events concerning the Soviet Union in the three newspapers during the 13 months studied included arms issues such as the Strategic Arms Reduction Talks (START), the agreement on intermediate-range nuclear forces (INF), the antiballistic missile (ABM) treaty that was signed in 1972, and the Strategic Defense Initiative (SDI). They also included the Moscow summit, Gorbachev's glasnost and perestroika policies, the Afghan pullout, Gorbachev's New York City visit, and the earthquake in Armenia.

The general direction in reporting these events tended to be more neutral and favorable than unfavorable (see Table 8.1).

Soviet reports in *The New York Times* and the *Washington Post* were basically neutral. However, the coverage of the Soviet Union in the *Los Angeles Times* was slightly negative. Sixty-two percent of the sample was neutral or favorable, and 38 percent received unfavorable treatment.

Most of the reports were written by staff writers and special contributors, and very few stories were based on information from the news agencies. Seventy-two percent of *The New York Times* stories were by staff writers, followed by 21 percent by contributors and 7 percent by wire services. In the *Washington Post,* 85 percent of the reports were made by staff writers, followed by contributors with 13 percent and wire services with 2 percent each (see Table 8.2).

Table 8.2. Sources of Stories

Source	New York Times	Washington Post	Los Angeles Times	Combined	Average
Staff Writers	72	85	58	215	71.7%
Contributors	21	13	28	62	20.7%
Wire services	7	2	14	23	7.6%
Total	100	100	100	300	100.0%

Table 8.3. Types of Stories

Type	New York Times	Washington Post	Los Angeles Times	Combined	Average
Straight news	51	63	45	159	53.0%
Columns	28	20	33	81	27.0%
Editorials	14	8	16	38	12.7%
Features	5	6	6	17	5.7%
Others	2	3	—	5	1.6%
Total	100	100	100	300	100.0%

With respect to the type of stories, more than half of the articles were written as straight news (53 percent). Columns and editorials accounted for 27 percent and 12.7 percent respectively. Feature stories came in fourth with 5.7 percent (see Table 8.3).

The category most heavily covered by the three newspapers was Mikhail Gorbachev's reform movement, with 28.4 percent. Political reform was next with 18.7 percent, and economic reform followed with 9.7 percent. The Moscow summit in June 1988 and Gorbachev's visit to the United States in December 1988 brought the U.S. media's attention to the policies of glasnost and perestroika, policies Gorbachev inititated and advocated.

Reports on the military ranked second in the analysis, representing 27.3 percent of the total 300 articles. Next came diplomatic stories which accounted for 9.7 percent. The human rights category ranked fourth with 8.3 percent (see Table 8.4).

Reports on Soviet Internal Affairs: Political Reforms

The New York Times

Glasnost and perestroika. Glasnost (openness) and perestroika (restructuring) were generally applauded but skeptics and critics remained wary. Almost

Table 8.4. Categories of Stories

Category	New York Times	Washington Post	Los Angeles Times	Combined	Average
Political reform	19	13	24	56	18.7%
Economic reform	3	8	18	29	9.7%
Military	28	44	10	82	27.3%
Diplomatic	16	12	1	29	9.7%
Human rights	9	4	12	25	8.3%
Government corruption	1	2	2	5	1.7%
Ethnic	1	2	17	20	6.7%
Disaster	2	1	3	6	2.0%
Cultural	7	1	9	17	5.7%
Science	5	3	—	8	2.6%
Others	9	10	4	23	7.6%
Total	100	100	100	300	100.0%

80 percent of the *Times*'s stories about Soviet political reform were either favorable or neutral, with only 20 percent unfavorable. An example of acknowledging changes but keeping wary is columnist A. M. Rosenthal's column titled "Formerly, the Evil Empire" on June 3, 1988:

> Mr. Gorbachev is bringing important changes to the Soviet Union . . . but it is a serious moral and political error for the United States to commit itself now to a man who is still the dictator of the most powerful totalitarian nation in the world.

Human rights. The issue of human rights remains a thorny one in the Soviet-U.S. relationship. Out of the nine reports on human rights, a little over half were unfavorable, 22 percent favorable, and the rest neutral. The *Times* report on October 14, 1988, quoted U.S. State Department spokesman Charles Redman as saying that the Soviets must take significant steps to improve their human rights performance before the United States would agree to a human rights conference in Moscow. The Soviet government, Redman claimed, was holding 250 to 300 political prisoners.

On May 20 an editorial, "One Man's Glasnost," noted Soviet improvements in human rights:

> The official press is far livelier. Independent groups proliferate. Once forbidden works are published. New writings push into uncharted territory. Mr. Gorbachev said that openness was essential because, without popular criticism and analysis, official abuse would never be prevented or corrected.

Natural calamities and corruption. The content and tone of two sample reports on the earthquake in Soviet Armenia were favorable to the Soviet image. As for corruption, a neutral image was presented.

The *Times* ran a front-page story December 9 on the quake, titled "Quake in Soviet Armenia; Gorbachev Flies Home from U.S." A large photo showed victims receiving medical treatment in Yerevan, the capital of Armenia. "Relief aid and workers rushed to the area from all over the Soviet Union, bearing medical supplies, blankets, tents and blood," the story read.

The other report about the quake said Soviet television coverage showed no buildings that had escaped unscathed. "The footage of the disaster was broadcast with unusual speed," the story read. "Mr. Gorbachev's statement was the first to give any clue to the human cost of the tragedy."

The *Washington Post*

Political and economic reform. Reports on Soviet political reform ranked second in the story category, occupying 13 percent of the articles. Out of 13 political stories, 6 (46 percent) were neutral, 5 (38 percent) favorable, and 2 (15 percent) unfavorable. But the two unfavorable stories were carried on the front pages of April 20 and November 25, each with four-column-wide headlines and each more than 20 column inches long. The favorable and neutral stories received comparatively less attention.

One editorial on June 29 said Gorbachev's intentions were clear: Political reform—meaning keeping the party in power but putting it into a more competitive environment—was the key to the general transformation he had in mind. The editorial indicated that the United States would "wait and see" on Soviet political reform: "It is forward and backward and side-ways in Moscow, with the outcome unclear. Just to see astonishing, long-dormant issues take life is to realize that Mikhail Gorbachev has brought his country to a place it has not been before."

Neutral and unfavorable news reports on Soviet political reform were found mostly during the period between November 1988 and January 1989. From these reports, we can see that the *Post* was interested in the Soviet domestic situation, the Soviet Communist party, and people's reaction to the political reform, especially their negative reactions.

Eight reports on Soviet economic reform were found in the *Washington Post*. Seven were over 15 column inches long. Four were columns, one was a news analysis, and three were straight news. Four of these stories were neutral, three unfavorable, and only one favorable. The average attention score of the eight reports was a low 1.8. None of them appeared with photos or on the front page or was treated as a top story.

Some interesting comments can be found in a column titled "Can Gorba-nomics Turn the Soviets Into Closet Capitalists?" According to the columnist, the rise of Mikhail Gorbachev surely signals the end of the contest between capitalism and communism, but Gorbachev's economic system can't keep up. It has trouble motivating people and promoting innovation. Perestroika, warned the columnist, may be an attempt to do the impossible, to introduce capitalist practices into a system whose ideology and institutions reject capitalism. "Gorba-nomics" was given as the context for the decision to cut Soviet military strength by 500,000 troops. Less military spending would help by permitting production of more consumer goods, wrote the columnist, who added that defense cutbacks were "a stop gap," and the problem was with the Soviet system itself. A Soviet economist was quoted as saying:

> No economic reform can work without political reform. Economic reform leads to decentralization. There is pressure to replace incompetent managers who are appointed for political reasons. The party loses influence. You get more groups demanding changes in laws and regulations.

The article concluded:

> Gorbachev's ambition makes him bolder on the world stage. He needs foreign policy successes to strengthen him at home. He also needs time. Gorba-nomics may fail completely. With luck, it might produce major economic gains by the mid-1990s. Nations don't change overnight. It's not easy to turn millions of communists into closet capitalists.

The general impression of the reports on Soviet economic reform is that more resistance to perestroika comes from inside the Soviet Union and more criticism of communism from outside the country.

Human rights. Articles about the human rights issue frequently appeared in the *Post*. Four articles, including two editorial columns, were chosen to see how the United States viewed this issue. The reports tended to be favorable or neutral.

One column on May 10 said, "It was a substantial achievement for American diplomacy that the Soviets have recognized human rights as a legitimate issue of US-Soviet relations." The column added:

> For the first time, Soviet officials have begun taking questions on human rights abuses. Slowly but steadily, about half of the political prisoners have been released. The rate of emigration has gone up. Advocacy on behalf of wronged Soviet citizens has become a routine element of the State Department's work.

Just like generals or diplomats, Soviet dissidents have begun measuring time by counting superpower summits.

Another column, "A Human Rights Success," on June 3, quoted a Soviet refusenik as saying, "There is no violation of human rights in the Soviet Union. They just don't exist here."

The *Los Angeles Times*

Political and economic reform. A number of articles that welcomed glasnost gave Gorbachev much credit for it. One titled "The Year the Weather Turned in Moscow" on January 3, 1989, said:

Unlike Leonid I. Brezhnev, who always played safe and whose highest ambition appeared to be to die in office at a ripe old age, Gorbachev is playing for higher stakes. He wants not only office but also power—the power to reconstruct the Soviet system.

At the heart of that system, in Moscow, Gorbachev has already made an amazing amount of progress—not in turning around the faltering Soviet economy (a longer-term task) but in changing the balance of power and influence at the center and in making a significant start with political reforms. . . . It would be difficult to deny that Gorbachev had been the most outstanding world leader of 1988. (Sec. 2, p. 7)

The Soviet progress in permitting freedom of speech was reported favorably in the *Los Angeles Times.* "Today there are no forbidden subjects for the Soviet people. They have begun to criticize, privately and publicly, Soviet foreign policy and Lenin—two of the last sacred cows standing for what is left of the old Soviet ideology," said an article titled "A Nation Where No One's Content."

The *Los Angeles Times* expressed lingering doubts on whether Gorbachev would succeed because he was challenging the basic Marxist ideology on which Soviet society had been built. They also carried criticism from Andrei D. Sakharov, who was a leading human rights activist, about Gorbachev's new power. Sakharov said that allowing one person to head both the Communist party and the government was "just insanity." Some stories related Gorbachev as a modern-day czar concentrating power that would exceed even that established by Stalin.

A worsening of shortages of food and consumer goods, lengthening lines for what little was available, and mounting discontent among the public was the general picture of the Soviet economy the *Los Angeles Times* showed its readers. Several articles blamed the Soviet economic system for the situation. They said that the elimination of private ownership and central planning caused the near-total absence of accountability and stifled initiative and innovation from factory floors to ministries.

To enlist public support for his reforms, Gorbachev changed Marxist thought, replacing "from each according to his ability, to each according to his needs" with "to each according to what he produces and nothing for those who produce not," the *Times* said. The paper concluded,

> As a result, central planning is being shifted to a market economy. Perestroika intends to create a viable price system so that managers can be held accountable for producing goods that people want. If an enterprise does well, producing goods more efficiently, then it should receive benefits; if it does poorly, it should suffer the consequences.

An article, "For Perestroika, Mikhail the Good May Have to Become Mikhail the Great," points to a number of flaws:

> [M]arket *perestroika* has its problems. 'Price reforms' rarely mean price cuts; prices for subsidized Soviet consumers have already begun to rise—without significant improvements in quality or availability. Ordinary Soviets are left with the bittersweet taste of *glasnost,* an increased ability to read about how bad things are. (January 15, 1989, Sec. 5, pp. 2, 6)

The official disclosure of the Soviet deficit was treated as the top story of the day in an article titled "$59-Billion Soviet Deficit in '89 Seen." Since the end of World War II, the Soviet government had always maintained that state expenditures were fully covered by its revenues and that it even had a surplus each year, the article said. Now for the first time the Soviet Union disclosed in public that the budget deficit had begun to increase in the mid-1970s and reached a peak of nearly $61 billion in 1985. The article estimated that the deficit would be $59 billion in 1989.

Human rights. The situation of human rights in the Soviet Union has greatly improved, but more action needs to be taken, the *Times* suggested. As a result of international criticism about the misuse of psychiatric treatment for political reasons in the Soviet Union and the recent mounting Soviet press coverage of the "lawlessness" behind the walls of psychiatric institutions, the Russian Federal Soviet Republic, the largest of the Soviet Union's 15 republics, rewrote its laws to make it a crime to commit "a patently healthy person" to a mental hospital.

A story on May 28 comparing the amount of personal freedom allowed at that time with conditions three years ago said that encouraging and startling differences could be found in the Soviet Union. "These changes are far more than cosmetic, but also far less than fundamental," the story said.

In a talk with the leader of the Russian Orthodox Church, Gorbachev was quoted as saying, "Believers have the full right to express their conviction with dignity." But the Soviet Union continued to persecute religious activities other than those officially authorized by the state, primarily the Russian Orthodox Church, the *Times* said.

In December, the Soviet Union disclosed its plan to drop the punishments of banishment and internal exile that had frequently been used to silence political dissidents. An article titled "New Soviet Code Will End Banishment, Internal Exile" reported this news with some encouraging facts:

> The new philosophy has already been put into effect, with the early release in the past 18 months of an estimated 620,000 prisoners, about a third of the whole Soviet prison population, most of whom were jailed for ordinary crimes. The elimination of internal exile and banishment, however, is particularly symbolic of the new era that Gorbachev hopes the reforms will bring. (December 17, 1988, pp. 1, 20)

The *Los Angeles Times* also reported the new tone of Reagan's praising the Soviets on human rights issues. The story about it began: "President Reagan, abandoning his harsh criticism of the Kremlin, credited the Soviet Union today with making progress on human rights and said gradual improvements are better than 'no change at all.'" The human rights changes in the Soviet Union were welcomed in the *Times,* but the paper urged the Soviet government to put their promises into practice.

Ethnic problems. "The claim that there are no ethnic conflicts in the Soviet Union is a myth—and a pernicious one too; those conflicts do exist and their number grows," the *Times* said in its story "Social Conflict in the Soviet Union." Soviet centralization guarantees stagnation, but Gorbachev's decentralization risks a rise of nationalism in various republics of the Soviet Union, the article said.

On February 11, hundreds of thousands of people filled the streets in the Armenian capital of Yerevan demanding an end to Azerbaijani control over the predominately Armenian Nagorno-Karabakh region. The turbulence took 34 lives and injured 247 others. This demand later was denounced as "anti-socialist" in *Pravda,* the Soviet official newspaper. In an editorial titled "Back to Basics in Armenia," the *Times* said:

What the Armenians seek is the return of Nagorno-Karabakh, an enclave that was once part of their republic and that is still populated primarily by Christian Armenians, but that was incorporated nearly 65 years ago into largely Muslim Azerbaijan on Joseph Stalin's order. (May 23, 1988, Sec. 2, p. 6)

Bilateral Military Relations

The New York Times

International life after World War II had been characterized by the confrontation between the Soviet Union and the United States and the intensifying arms race, regional conflicts, and antagonistic ideologies. But the survey of *The New York Times* reports on Soviet-U.S. ties found that traditional military terms like "first surgical strike," "thrust capability," and "military superiority" had largely given way to "propitious omen," "military balance," and "defensive posture." Forty-three percent of the 28 military stories were favorable, 50 percent were neutral, and only 7 percent were unfavorable.

The *Times* adopted a positive attitude toward the treaty on intermediate-range nuclear forces (INF) in its editorial on March 30, 1988, the day the Senate Foreign Relations Committee was scheduled to vote on the treaty. "The Euromissile treaty is remarkable for its extensive verification procedures," the editorial said. "The Soviet Union could still cheat—but not in militarily significant ways." The editorial, titled "Some Arms Cheating May Not Matter," pointed out that "to insist on airtight verification is to insist on no agreement."

Tom Wicker wrote in his column of June 28, 1988, "The United States is confronting a new but perhaps final 'moment of opportunity' to meet the Soviet Union halfway in putting an end to an arms race and a cold war that hamper the security and prosperity of both." Another article, "Seize the Moment: A Rare Chance for Arms Control," said, "Mr. Gorbachev has made the major arms control concessions. . . . These proposals might lead to desirable force reductions and greater stability in Europe, hence to economic relief and political gains for both sides."

On February 12, when a Soviet frigate bumped a U.S. warship in the Black Sea, it set off a public alarm. The *Times* issued an editorial entitled "A Serious Scrape, But Still a Scrape." It called the incident "manageable, a small piece of a complex relationship," and "one episode in a longtime policy disagreement." The U.S.-Soviet difference on free passage is only a piece in the bigger mosaic of relations between the two nations, the editorial went on. Those who gravely seize on this incident to resist Senate ratification of the Euromissile treaty are overreacting. Besides ritualistic diplomatic representations, the editorial said, "Each side hastened to add: Let's not make too much of this." It described the incident as part of a competitive relationship to which "both sides are bringing growing maturity." The editorial indicated a desire by the *Times* to play down the military friction in the incident and to refrain from criticizing only the Soviet Union.

A *Times* editorial lauded Gorbachev's notion that "the common interests of mankind" take precedence over class struggle, saying that "his more constructive tone challenges the West to examine its own ideological rigidities." According to a *Times* report, White House officials portrayed the Reagan-Gorbachev summit as a success because it helped to stabilize the relationship between Washington and Moscow. The paper's evaluations of the summit were mostly very positive.

U.S. Defense Secretary Frank Carlucci and Soviet Defense Minister Dmitri Yazov were reported to have watched a mock battle at an army base outside Moscow. Carlucci and his entourage were the first Westerners to see the latest Soviet long-range strategic bomber, known in the West as the Blackjack, up close. "The fact . . . was a reflection not only of changing relations between the superpowers but also of Mikhail Gorbachev's mastery over the military," *Times* columnist Philip Taubman commented. If a senior Soviet military officer had suggested two or three years ago that the American secretary of defense be invited to inspect the most advanced Russian warplanes, he probably would have been sent to a remote Siberian army base, if not a mental ward, Taubman said.

The *Washington Post*

The direction in reporting on Soviet military and defense issues was more neutral and favorable than unfavorable. A column with the headline "START Can Be Verified Too" in the *Washington Post* on March 23 expressed a positive U.S. attitude toward the INF and START treaties: "The INF Treaty has received widespread support, in part because of its precedent-setting verification measures." At the outset of the strategic arms limitation talks, the column read:

> [T]he Soviets refused to divulge even the names of their military systems. Now they are providing names, places, numbers and infrastructure. They are also allowing inspections to confirm the data provided. INF verification provisions cannot ensure the accuracy of these data, but they make it harder and more expensive for the Soviets to cheat.

Another editorial, with the headline "Too Hungry for START," on May 27, read, "What's wrong with START? The numbers. Arms control feels good only if the numbers are right. In fact, START cuts reduce stability."

The editorial said that official U.S. position on START was to ban mobile missiles, because the United States considered it very hard to determine whether its opponents were keeping with the required numbers. If you can't find the mobile missiles, the editorial continued, surely you can't target them. This means that you cannot wipe them out in a surprise attack and that they are always there for retaliation; they are a permanent deterrent to nuclear war.

The U.S. Senate's moaning before ratification made the START treaty difficult to achieve during Reagan's term in office. That is why there was no arms breakthrough during the Moscow summit. Reagan predicted three months before the summit that the "time is too limited" for a strategic arms treaty in Moscow. Despite this, the *Post* took a neutral or favorable tone in most of the reports on the summit.

The neutral stories on the Moscow summit were reports on Gorbachev's reaction to the summit. The article "Missed Chances at Summit" on June 2 said, "Gorbachev complained that the Reagan administration was not prepared to go even further in the relationship" and that "more could have been achieved" at the summit.

As for the "peaceful coexistence" set forth by Gorbachev at the Moscow summit, it did not receive the expected welcome. Reports on this point in the *Post* leaned toward an unfavorable view. The paper said, "U.S. Secretary of State George Shultz and other officials reacted negatively to the proposed declaration of 'peaceful coexistence.'" A U.S. official called it "ambiguous, freighted with the baggage of the past," the *Post* reported.

An unfavorable feature story, "The Superpowers Struggle Over 'Peaceful Coexistence,'" on June 3, said that the words in Gorbachev's proposed statement "sound positive to many people, but to U.S. diplomats and others familiar with the struggles of the past, the words take on a special and, for some, worrisome meaning."

Beginning in mid-July, there were more unfavorable and neutral stories on the issue of the slow Soviet troop pullout from Afghanistan. Of eight articles selected from the period between July 24 and December 9, four were unfavorable and four were neutral. One major unfavorable story, "Soviet Said to Slow Afghan Troop Pullout," which ran on the front page on July 24, reported U.S. officials' concern that the Soviet Union would not meet an August 15 deadline for removing half of its troops from Afghanistan and that the Soviet Union had sent back 10,000 troops to defend Kabul.

There were more Soviet stories in the *Post* after December 1988, when three major events caught the attention of the world. One was Gorbachev's announcement that he would substantially reduce the Warsaw Pact's ability to launch a surprise attack on the West. The other two were Gorbachev's visit to New York City and the Armenian earthquake. Reports during this period were numerous.

Reports on the Soviet cuts were more neutral and unfavorable than favorable. This was quite different from the previous reports on the INF and START treaties and the Moscow summit in the first half of 1988, which were more favorable or neutral than unfavorable.

An editorial in December, "Gorbachev's Cuts: Gift or Gambit," expressed the real U.S. concern. It said Gorbachev's announcement that the Soviet Union would reduce 500,000 troops and six tank divisions in Eastern Europe could not be dismissed so easily:

> Gorbachev has presented an opportunity to seize his initiative and use it as a measure to produce a less threatening, more stable and positive relationship. But while grateful for a unilateral step long overdue, America must remain guarded as well. We must resist the temptation to make a reciprocal gesture in the form of troop and equipment cuts in Europe at this time. We must ask: What tanks will be eliminated? Will they be destroyed or simply removed, so they might return another day? How will these reductions be verified?

Regarding the Soviet military and defense, the *Post* carried more neutral and favorable reports in the first half of 1988, but more neutral and unfavorable items in the second half of the year on some major issues such as the INF and START treaties, the Moscow summit, the Soviet troop pullout from Afghanistan, and Gorbachev's troop reduction announcement.

Diplomatic activity is the third largest category, which accounts for 12 percent of the stories. Such stories mainly deal with U.S.-Soviet diplomatic activities and bilateral relations. Among the 12 stories in the *Post,* 8 were favorable (67 percent) and 4 neutral (33 percent). None of them was unfavorable.

The reports on diplomatic activities can be divided into two periods. One is from mid-November to mid-December, when Gorbachev was about to visit or was visiting the United States. Nine of the 12 reports (75 percent) covered Gorbachev's New York City visit in December. The other period covered late May and early June, when Reagan went to Moscow for the summit.

Reports on Reagan's Moscow tour were given great attention in the *Post,* and most of the stories were definitely positive. This is shown by a page-one article on June 1 with a six-column-wide headline saying "Reagan Sees Exciting, Hopeful Times Under Gorbachev." The article quoted Reagan as saying:

> Nothing would please my heart more than in my lifetime to see American and Soviet diplomats grappling with the problem of trade disputes rather than military disputes between America and a growing, exuberant, exporting Soviet Union that had opened up to economic freedom and growth.

On relations between the Soviet Union and the United States, Gorbachev said, "Relations between our two countries have overcome a long drawn-out period of confrontation to reach an acceptable level from which it is now easier to move forward."

More positive opinions appeared in the period before, during, and after Gorbachev's tour of New York City in early December. A Reagan-Bush-Gorbachev session in New York was reported as a "continuous mini-summit." A report on December 9 said Reagan credited the Soviets with improving relations. Reagan said the United States and Soviet Union could become allies again as they had been in World War II, and this would "all depend on them (the Soviets)" and could happen if it became "definitely established that they no longer are following the expansionist policy."

During Gorbachev's New York visit, a devastating earthquake struck Armenia and cut short Gorbachev's trip. Before Gorbachev's departure, Reagan reportedly told his counterpart that "if there is any way in which we—the United States—can be of assistance, either bilaterally or through the international community, please let me know."

A front-page article on December 9 with the headline "Grim Gorbachev Leaves Early, Praises Visit Result" expressed Gorbachev's "deep gratitude" and "profound appreciation" to Reagan and Bush for their offer of assistance to victims of the earthquake. Gorbachev said, "I would like to thank them and thank the American people for those feelings of sympathy and for their readiness to give assistance in this difficult hour."

The *Los Angeles Times*

During the 13 months studied, the Soviet Union made significant progress in its withdrawal from Afghanistan and in arms reductions. Some of the stories in the *Times* covered these changes favorably. In December, Gorbachev announced that the Soviet Union would unilaterally cut its military forces by 10 percent, reduce its forces in Eastern Europe, and pull its troops out of Mongolia and Asia.

As Gorbachev announced the removal of 50,000 troops, some critics raised doubts, suggesting that the Soviets would take the troops from Eastern Europe and relocate them in the rear area. "Sadly, the vestige of mistrust and negative stereotypes linger on," said an article titled "Soviet Military Is Proving Commitment to Troops Cut and a Defensive Posture." "These troops will be released from military service and the units being pulled out will be disbanded—not redeployed to the rear." The article praised the Soviet effort in cutting its force, saying:

The Soviet Union is taking practical measures to demonstrate its commitment to defensive defense, and is even prepared to widen these measures to cover its navy. . . . The developments of the past few years have raised hopes that what was once impossible is possible now.

The Soviet plan of a chemical-arms cut and the destruction of three SS-20 intermediate-range missiles were all reported in the *Times*. Some articles, however, expressed the fear that the Soviets were moving to produce more sophisticated weapons.

"The CIA believes that the Soviet weapons procurement leveled off in the mid-70s. But they also see a big increase in military research and development and a growing emphasis on higher quality weapons," said an article titled "Guns and Butter Loom as Glasnost's Big Hurdle." "It is arguable, therefore, that even if significant reductions are made in missiles and even conventional forces, the savings won't go into the civilian economy but into new and better weapons down the line," the article said.

Conclusion

The Soviet Union underwent many radical changes during the 13-month period of this study. In the domestic political arena, Gorbachev consolidated his power in the Politburo. He became the head of both the Communist party and the government, a situation that had been banned by the party Cental Committee since the removal of Nikita Khrushchev in 1964. Yegor K. Ligachev, the principal conservative voice in the Politburo and Gorbachev's main political rival, was shifted from overseeing ideology to running agriculture. Andrei A. Gromyko and three other longtime members at the top of the party hierarchy were retired to make way for Gorbachev's supporters.

To renew the momentum of Soviet productivity, Gorbachev called on the party to yield its monopoly on power to the government, economic enterprises, and social institutions. In one of his most fundamental reforms, he urged that the party be put under the Soviet constitution and legal system.

Along with this, a vast array of new laws have been drafted. Crimes for "anti-Soviet behavior," for instance, will be taken off the books or the penalties for them reduced significantly. The philosophy behind all the new laws is to uphold the rights of people to carry out whatever activities are not harmful to society. The old code of prohibition will be changed to a new code of freedom.

To press further ahead, Gorbachev proposed far-reaching constitutional changes: establishment of a full-time, two-chamber legislature headed by an executive president, and a whole electoral system to encourage contested elections with true campaigning and secret ballots. All these dramatic changes have caught the attention of the three American newspapers.

The New York Times. The *Times* especially did a good job in portraying a fair, balanced image of the Soviet Union in the 13-month period. During that time, two U.S.-Soviet summits took place, the INF treaty took effect, and Soviets began to end their nine-year occupation of Afghanistan.

This study demonstrated that *New York Times* reports on the Soviet Union basically were objective and free of political prejudices and resentment. They contributed much to improving the Soviet image among Americans—from the "evil empire" of the Stalin and Brezhnev eras to "a more trustworthy and less threatening country."

The American media have in the past depicted the Soviet leader as an enemy and even labeled him a "Soviet devil." Now instead, Soviet leader Gorbachev is termed a "supreme realist" with the support of the people. The image of a country such as the Soviet Union largely depends on its paramount leader, who has the final say on almost all major policy decisions. It seems necessary, therefore, to take a close look at Gorbachev, the Soviet leader, as portrayed by *The New York Times.*

The findings of the study show that *The New York Times* has given substantial coverage to the Soviet Union. Its pervasive reporting has been effective and credible in rendering a complex and true image of the Soviet Union. The results have also shown that the *Times*'s direction in covering Soviet news changed as the Soviet Union began undergoing rapid political and social reforms.

The Washington Post. The coverage of the Soviet Union in the *Washington Post* presents a positive or neutral image of the Soviet Union rather than a negative one. The Soviet military and defense received much more coverage in the *Post* than any other topics. Reports on specific issues such as the INF and START treaties, the Moscow summit, Soviet political reform, U.S.-Soviet relations, human rights, and the earthquake in Armenia were mostly favorable or neutral.

The United States welcomes the Soviet Union's arms reductions, but it is still skeptical about its less confrontational stance, according to the *Post.* The United States believes that the Soviet Union might become more aggressive in pursuit of information, especially high-tech information, *Post* stories suggest.

Less favorable reports were found on the Soviet troop pullout from Afghanistan, the cuts of 500,000 Soviet troops in Eastern Europe, and the Soviet economic reform.

The United States has a "wait and see" attitude regarding Gorbachev and his promised reforms, the *Post* suggests. The Moscow summit was considered one of the most important events of 1988. A *Post* article said the desire to end the Cold War, which is defined as a combination of the arms race and openly hostile East-West relations, could be felt through this summit.

On the issue of human rights, the *Post* points out that small but significant progress has taken place in the Soviet Union, but there is still a long way to go in this area. The development of civil society and the right to monitor and publicize human rights abuses inside the Soviet Union is more important than admitting the problem to the outside world, the *Post* suggests. It says that legitimizing human rights monitors should become the next stage of glasnost.

The Los Angeles Times. The *L. A. Times* carried a number of articles praising the changes in the Soviet Union and indicating Gorbachev would succeed in his reforms. But some stories pointed out that the Soviet system and Marxism are wrong. Without abandoning the old beliefs and traditional practice, the *Times* said, the reforms would be meaningless and would go nowhere.

Glasnost and perestroika are in for difficult times. The *Times* in general expressed its hope that Gorbachev would succeed for the sake of the Soviet people.

9
Mass Media: Stereotypes and Structure

ELENA ANDROUNAS

Perestroika in the Soviet Union is a new revolution, bringing many radical changes in our way of life. The media are among the most influential forces in this environment because of the policy of perestroika. But the media are not just instruments of change; they are also subject to change themselves.

Although newspapers have retained their political affiliation, the responsibility for their content has shifted to the editors, and this has created a wide political spectrum of publications from radical to conservative. Their circulation has become an important indicator of public opinion, not only through the growth and decline of numbers of subscribers but also through massive cancellations of subscriptions to protest individual articles.

In television programming there have been some exciting changes, but fewer than in the printed media. The programming for the two national channels, one national educational channel, and numerous local channels is still centrally supervised by the Gosteleradio, which acts as a virtual broadcasting monopoly with respect to the distribution of frequencies for the broadcast media. A wide range of opinion is not likely to be heard under this broadcasting system.

To participate fully in perestroika, then, the media also require revolutionary change. We now acknowledge that we are part of a "world civilization" and that we can learn from the experience of others. As we receive more information and gain more experience, we must also seek ways to initiate the structural changes that will allow the media to represent that diversity.

A personal experience illustrates the media situation between the United States and the Soviet Union only a decade ago. To prepare for my visit to the United States, I had read American periodicals in the Moscow libraries. But when I arrived, I felt that somehow my country had disappeared from the map of the world. The paucity of media references to the Soviet Union, particularly regarding everyday life, stood out in my mind. One television news item was devoted to the strong frosts in Moscow and another to the shortage of mascara in the Moscow shops. An animated cartoon featured pigs dressed in costumes similar to Russian military uniforms dancing in Red Square. In contrast, I did not consider *From Russia With Love* as hostile as our media had described it.

My own ideas of the United States, probably typical of the time for most regular readers of the Soviet press, also turned out to be inadequate. The belief that the vast majority of the population were oppressed and exploited while a handful were wealthy and powerful turned out to be a stereotype. Though of course those extremes were visible, the reality was much more diversified and colorful. Yet overall the Soviet feeling toward the United States, despite its stereotype, was of sympathetic moral solidarity with American workers, not hostility.

Although each country's media system was radically different from the other, biases and distortions were typical of both systems. These biases could not be explained purely by ideological bases, or by the "iron curtain" phenomenon. I would argue that the structure of the media in each country, which is itself a reflection of the material bases of ideology, influences in many ways and to a large degree the content of the media.

Mass media structure is a very complicated configuration that involves the quality and quantity of national, international, and local media organizations; media relationships with the government; economic and financial arrangements and management; relations with audiences; news sources; information flows; technological resources; legal status; and access to the public. I shall concentrate on key aspects of media structures that are crucial to the functioning of the mass media and are of real importance for the development of images and stereotypes.

Today of course the situation is altered by the changed political climate and the increased media attention given to each country by the other. Each country is not always portrayed without sympathy, even if it is not always shown in an attractive light. But the structure of the media has remained essentially the same in both countries, and certain conditions that encouraged the old stereotypes are still firmly in place. So although old stereotypes might seemingly be less visible, the changes may represent more of a superficial trend than one supportable throughout the media system or on a long-term basis. I would like to examine two aspects of a mass media system that have a strong impact on determining its content—its technological base and its organization.

Technological Base

Over the last 10 to 20 years the rapid development of new technologies has given information an existence independent of the channel through which it is transmitted. Whether through a newspaper, television program, fax machine, or computer network, information has become a commodity for distribution. Two major consequences of the new technologies are (a) the elimination of obstacles to the news flow from source to recipient; and (b) the consolidation, unification, and transformation of the various mass media into an indivisible information processing system.

These changes influence the structure of the media. With some of the new technologies—like photocopiers and fax machines—there are interpreters of checkpoints in the chain of the media systems. Voice-activated computers and electronic photography will no doubt further minimize distortions of the message between sender and receiver. The networking of communication channels even across political borders has made possible increasingly large information systems capable of generating and distributing more and more information.

But is it really the amount of information that is increasing or is it the number of channels? Information is not a disposable commodity as much as it is a reusable one. And the increasing number of channels that are linked to each other may simply be fulfilling a service function by customizing information in a form most suitable for a variety of receivers.

In the United States this trend is illustrated by *USA Today.* Although this newspaper generates some of its own information, in large part it is based on the vast information network of the numerous Gannett publications. *USA Today* in turn recycles its information to the Gannett Company, to a number of its own electronic and audio information services. This phenomenon is by no means unique. The television industry shows similar trends toward consolidation of resources, both through cable consortia and, more slowly, among producers of syndicated television programs.

Larger and larger organizations seem to be increasingly advantageous for the capital and efficiency necessary to obtain, package, and distribute information on a large scale. This type of system not only customizes information according to the receiver's ability to pay for the new technologies—owning a computer or renting cable access—but also leads to the standardization of information in the name of efficiency. Media conglomerates, through multiple channels of the same format, also encourage the efficient transmission of stereotypes.

I have been a longtime critic of media monopolies and media concentration, and I remain critical of them. But I also believe now that the concentration of capital in large corporate organizations provides a unique opportunity for the realization of the new technologies' potential in a most effective way. If these corporations did not exist, they would have to be invented. Consolidation of different media in the framework of the same corporation creates an optimum organizational structure for servicing the needs of the consumers of the information age by allowing for the newest technological achievements at the cheapest possible price. The price for the access to information remains high, however, and the information explosion also implies a new social division between the information rich and the information poor. The monopolization of the access to the media and the news flow remains a complicated problem that I believe the USSR can solve, but I do not think that we can penetrate the information age without diversified organizations.

In the Soviet Union the mass media structure is quite unlike the American one and the problems we face are quite different. Whereas the U.S. media are competing for the leisure time of the audience, in the Soviet Union the demand for media products is much greater than the supply. Although in Moscow there are five television channels, only one seventh of the population in other areas receives three or more channels. Video is a rarity, as is cable television. In radio only one of the four all-union programs covers almost all the country. Although there are national, regional, and local broadcasts, the number of broadcast stations is 10 times lower than in the United States and doesn't meet our needs.

For the print media the situation is more promising. We have 1,500 magazines with a combined circulation of about 200 million and a clear potential for growth. Newspapers, including all dailies and weeklies, number 8,300, with a circulation of 180 million as of 1989.

But these numbers do not provide an accurate picture, particularly for a nation of over 280 million people. The print industry is plagued by problems and accentuated by technological backwardness. Essentially there is no system of information in the country as a whole because of a lack of computers, data bases, or telecommunications networks to share information among regions except by way of scarce paper products, telephone calls, or telegraph. Although the regional basis of most publications allows for some plurality and independence, it also encourages regional isolation and limits national and international participation. Simply stated, much information exchange stops at the borders of the Soviet Union simply because there are no technological facilities to send and receive it.

Organization

The technological problems are compounded by organizational ones. Our informational backwardness is reinforced by the bureaucratic structure, sometimes called a command-administrative system, which runs each media organization separately. Unlike the United States, where the media production and distribution systems are increasingly vertically and horizontally integrated, the Soviet media structure is in no way unified. It is a collection of separate media organizations void of any institutionally common economic or managerial structure. Radio in the Soviet Union has nothing to do with the press, the Ministry of Communications doesn't bother with television troubles, and so on. This situation might not be so bad if it meant only plurality and independence, but it also implies a disorderly supply of information and a kind of information starvation. Each sector tries to solve its problems on its own, with none of the advantages to be gained by pooling scarce resources or combining political clout. Meanwhile, the bureaucracy takes the profits of the various departments, particularly the press, and returns little in subsidies for development.

In other areas of our economy, bureaucratic obstacles are being eliminated and consortia are being formed, but not among the media. Instead, we still have various party organs that oversee and coordinate media operations with the type of infighting and territorial concerns that come from balancing local, regional, and national needs. The "top-down" orders have not allowed for an integrated or coordinated policy among the media organizations themselves.

The party initiated the processes of perestroika and glasnost that have made the media of our country exciting for the world at large. These policies have encouraged some dismantling of the old stereotypes. But without a more modernized media complex to take advantage of the information available, this process cannot effectively provide the rich information environment needed to sustain the effort and to help us participate in global issues. An informed and educated citizenry, the "human factor" of perestroika, is vital to its success.

To that end, we need to consider an overall approach to the mass media that still preserves their local and regional pluralities. We can begin by thinking of ways to remove the bureaucratic barriers to cooperation among media, perhaps by forming a data base as an integrator of information systems available to all. We also need more awareness of the horizontal relations among media to dismantle the destructive aspects of centralized, vertical control. Finally, we should carefully examine ways in which new technologies can be incorporated into the media system without repeating the centralized and standardized approach to information. These actions must be carefully studied and understood if we are to maintain the openness that the current era has created.

Modern media development involves serious and substantial capital investments. The concentration of capital makes new technological facilities and know-how available for new media ventures and new media structures. The globalization of the media that has involved the launching of global television and newspapers has been one of the most striking developments in the media world of the 1980s. The Soviet Union was a pioneer in direct television broadcasting but has not yet developed its own global television network. The United States Information Agency attempted to launch its Worldnet without much success. Rupert Murdoch's transnational News Corporation and Ted Turner's Cable News Network opened up their global networks and achieved considerable results where the U.S. government failed. Four global newspapers (the *International Herald Tribune, USA Today,* the *Wall Street Journal,* and the *Financial Times*) are being published by media corporations, three of them American. There is no Soviet global newspaper. The absence of the Soviet Union in the global media system is largely the result of the inadequate funding of media development. A Soviet global television network is in the making and will soon be available to world audiences, but the prospects of a Soviet global newspaper are very distant indeed.

The global factor is of extreme importance in the dissemination of images. The delivery of images and their availability influence their formation in many ways. The Soviet public's access to the *International Herald Tribune, USA Today,* and the Cable News Network, however limited it might be, is contributing to a better understanding of the United States and to more realistic images of America and Americans. But the American public's lack of exposure to the Soviet media does not help bring its images closer to Soviet realities—an illustration of media structures influencing images.

Structural differences of the two media systems determine to a large degree specific qualitative and substantial characteristics of images and stereotypes. The U.S. media system is basically audiovisual and based on the use of the information from data banks. Ninety million U.S. households (98 percent) have at least one television set, whereas the total circulation of U.S. dailies is about 62 million copies, or about 67 percent of the total number of 92 million households in the United States. The structure of American stereotypes is strongly influenced by television images, more visual and emotional and therefore more difficult to change. In the Soviet Union, the printed media (i.e., the daily newspapers) are much more important for the general public and the characteristics of Soviet images are mostly verbal, which means that they are more rational and flexible.

Another important feature of the U.S. media system is a well-developed television entertainment programming industry, as exemplified by the biggest media corporation of the world, Time-Warner. The reruns of old programs, some of which were highly politicized during the peaks of the Cold

War, are also a factor in promoting old stereotypes. These shows, sold at low prices on the international television markets, influence the world audiences' images of the Soviet Union. Data banks, which are so important for the American media and unfortunately are not developed in the Soviet Union, also to a great degree promote unification and standardization of information and images. In this way they are an important factor in creating stereotypes.

Globalization of media systems and of the flows of information throughout the world can contribute to both the unification and standardization of images if global media are monopolized by one country. If global media belong to the world community or a variety of countries, they can add to the enrichment, individualization, and pluralism of images of the world. The deficiencies at this stage in the Soviet global media system do not allow American audiences to get a Soviet version of events, or to get a closer look at Soviet life through the eyes of Soviet television or a Soviet newspaper. The strengthening of Soviet media structures and their improvements, which involve new capital investments, are of vital importance to the Soviet people. They can also contribute in a decisive way to a better understanding of our country in the various regions of the world and certainly in the United States.

Global communication systems already have been used to bridge the gap between the Soviet Union and the United States. Soviet-American spacebridges proved to be quite important in dismantling the enemy image, but the spacebridges were not efficient enough in providing a permanent and instant communication link between the two countries. Such a link is extremely important for the development of communication between the two nations on the level of world television, but even more important as a precaution against a surprise attack and as a measure of international security. The most efficient way of promoting international and national security in our two countries is through mutual interpenetration of the media that still play a vital role in keeping and promoting international security.

Mutual media interpenetration may be most effectively achieved through developing full-fledged Soviet and American global media structures, which will make instantly available to every citizen of our countries the realities of our lives. Every American and Soviet citizen will be able to keep an inquisitive eye on the house of his or her neighbor and as a result witness a much truer image. Developing interpenetrating global mass media structures in the Soviet Union and in the United States will eventually destroy enemy stereotypes and will become a mass media watch of national and international security.

10
Enemy Turned Partner: A Content Analysis of *Newsweek* and *Novoye Vremya*

ANDREI G. RICHTER

Rapid changes occurring in Soviet society are making us take a fresh look at our own country and at the entire world. These changes are transforming the image of the Soviet Union abroad. The people of today are witnesses to a great shift of values, interests, and directions. If this shift is genuine, then how are the new trends reflected in the columns of American and Soviet newsmagazines? The purpose of this study is to examine the portrayals of the Soviet Union in *Newsweek,* an American weekly newsmagazine, and the portrayals of the United States in *Novoye Vremya* (*New Times*), a Soviet weekly newsmagazine.

Design and Method

The method used for this study was content analysis. All the articles with corresponding content were divided into three large groups. The first group consisted of reports and features concentrating on Soviet or American internal affairs. The second group included stories covering foreign policy. Articles in the third group dealt with military issues such as the armed forces of the "likely enemy," its activities within the limits of the Warsaw Pact or the North Atlantic Treaty Organization, Warsaw Pact NATO balance of power, arms control talks, and the peace movement.

Content, including pictures and headings, was measured in square inches. Items less than one third of a page were not taken into account. The figures obtained were organized into the tables below. Quantitative content analysis was supplemented by qualitative analysis.

The magazines' content for the first halves of 1985, 1987, and 1989 was examined. The time limits include a period from the peak of the "stagnation years" to the present perestroika era. The whole body of the material studied

Table 10.1 *Newsweek* Soviet Stories

| | *1985* | | | *1987* | | | *1989* | | |
	sq. in.	*% of space*	*Cover Stories*	*sq. in.*	*% of space*	*Cover Stories*	*sq. in.*	*% of space*	*Cover Stories*
Internal affairs	2,270	30.1	1	2,840	44.3	0	3,560	41.2	1
Foreign policy	2,900	38.5	0	1,780	27.8	0	3,830	44.4	2
Military issues	2,360	31.4	1	1,790	27.9	1	1,240	14.4	0
Total	7,530	100.0	2	6,410	100.0	1	8,630	100.0	3

comprised 78 issues of *Novoye Vremya* and 76 issues of *Newsweek* (European edition). The comparison of the two magazines is valid because their type, volume, and size are very similar.

Analysis and Findings

Newsweek

Table 10.1 shows the results of the content analysis of Soviet-related stories in *Newsweek*.

The main conclusion here might be an increase in the prominence of reports on Moscow's domestic and foreign affairs owing to a general rise in space given to Soviet stories and a drop of interest in military issues. This increase would be even more noticeable if one took into account that more than a fifth of the Soviet-related content in the first half of 1985 appeared in a single special issue (1985, No. 12) devoted to the change of leadership in this country.

It should also be noted here that the general volume of Soviet-related content in the first half of 1989 reached 123 pages. That would make up approximately 2.5 out of 26 issues for the indicated period, or five full issues of *Newsweek* a year filled with only Soviet stories. With respect to the quality of the stories, see Table 10.2, which shows the distribution of the first two large groups of Soviet-related items into a number of categories.

The further glasnost goes and the more deeply embedded democratization becomes in the U.S.S.R., the more nervous are the well-rewarded propagandists of the different system. (*Novoye Vremya,* 1987, No. 13, p. 17)

Table 10.2 *Newsweek* Soviet Story Topics

Topic	1985 sq. in.	1985 % of space	1987 sq. in.	1987 % of space	1989 sq. in.	1989 % of space
News and commentary about Soviet internal affairs	2,270	100	2,840	100	3,560	100
Dissidents, Jewish emigration, KGB activities	100	4.4	1,060	37.3	210	5.9
Elections to and proceedings of the new parliament	—	0	—	0	930	26.1
Disasters	—	0	70	2.5	400	11.2
Ethnic conflicts	—	0	—	0	350	9.8
Science, technology, medicine	330	14.4	210	7.4	140	3.9
Art, culture, literature in/on USSR, sport	260	11.3	600	21.1	790	22.2
News and commentary on Soviet foreign policy	2,900	100	1,780	100	3,830	100
U.S.-Soviet relations	600	20.7	380	21.3	430	11.3
-Historical aspects	290	10.0	—	0	140	3.7
Covert actions and spy work by the KGB	770	26.6	—	0	—	0
Soviet relations with Cuba	—	0	—	0	400	10.4
Soviet relations with African countries	—	0	—	0	150	3.8
USSR and the Middle East	160	5.5	70	3.9	210	5.5
Relations with China and Japan	140	4.8	—	0	470	12.3
Soviet relations with Afghanistan	100	3.5	30	1.7	920	24.0
Relations with East European countries	350	12.1	480	27.0	410	10.7
Relations with other countries	560	19.3	350	19.7	70	1.8
East-West relations, ways to understand the Soviets	—	0	440	24.7	700	18.3

In discussing the portrayal of glasnost and perestroika in the pages of *Newsweek* I reject the above thesis. In my opinion the tone and trend of the reports became more objective and calm. Judge for yourself: Space given to items about KGB activities both at home and abroad, and about dissidents and Jewish emigration, decreased sharply. During the period studied, only two stories on these topics were printed in the newsmagazine: the first a rather positive interview with KGB Chairman Vladimir Kryuchkov (1989, No. 25); the second about problems and hopes of Soviet Jews at the transit township in Italy (1989, No. 9). Every report from the Soviet Union written by the *Newsweek* authors had positive coloring. But all those items shared a common mistake: Although approving of interior processes in our country, they considered them to be a "dismantling of communism."

> The symbol of our times is a statue of Karl Marx lying shattered in the marketplace. (*Newsweek,* 1989, No. 1)

While putting absolute trust in Mr. Gorbachev's words on other subjects, American mass media turn a deaf ear to his statements about restructuring (perestroika) and the strengthening of the USSR on the principles of socialism.

The study also shows that Americans are becoming less interested in Soviet science and technology. Coverage of culture increased, but this is attributable mainly to items about "American Russians." Also included under this topic—culture—is a six-page review of *The Russia House* by John le Carré (1989, No. 23). This book review, by the way, occupied more space than all reviews of Soviet literature in the studied period taken together.

Remembering her work in the USSR, *Newsweek*'s Moscow bureau chief from 1985 to 1988 writes:

> Within a four-year span, precisely as long as a one-term American president has to get his message across, the great Soviet communicator has felt the friendly weight of Ronald Reagan's arm around his shoulder in Red Square, topped the ranks of most-popular world leaders in opinion polls taken in western Europe, and transformed the Western stereotype of the Soviet Union as an Evil Empire. (Joyce Barnathan, "Gorbachev and the Press," *Gannett Center Journal,* Vol. 3, No. 2, Spring 1989)

Such a view of the Soviet image certainly influenced the way Moscow's foreign policy was covered by the magazine. Principal questions were put in an increased number of items, such as: How should we understand Soviet policy? How might it influence East-West relations? Different opinions were presented to the reader, from rigid ("A Better Record on Human Rights in Exchange for Economic Assistance," 1987, No. 9, p. 4) to euphoric ("The Dying of Communism," 1989, No. 26).

Many favorable reports dealt with the Soviet troop pullout from Afghanistan, among them a cover story (1989, No. 7). A 10-page report discussed Sino-Soviet relations on the eve of Mikhail Gorbachev's visit to China (1989, No. 21). As a rule, *Newsweek* gave substantial coverage of bilateral relations with Cuba, India, and other countries only in connection with Mr. Gorbachev's meetings with the respective state leaders.

To summarize the results of the Soviet-related content analysis:

(1) Coverage of interior processes within the USSR and of its foreign policy increased.

(2) Arms control was of less interest to U.S. readers, possibly because they believed that the Soviets were starting to disarm themselves and the details were not so interesting.

(3) KGB activities, which used to occupy a substantial space in *Newsweek,* either stopped or, in the editors' view, presented an unnecessary scar on the new face of the Soviet Union.

(4) As a consequence of the preceding point, disasters, accidents, and ethnic conflicts became the main focus of *Newsweek*'s coverage of the Soviet Union.

In general, in 1987 and especially in 1985, *Newsweek* readers could see a picture of an alien empire full of repression within the country and espionage outside its borders, a country with huge stocks of armaments and a grim foreign minister whose approval of an American proposal was viewed as an outstanding event. In 1989, the Soviet Union was treated in *Newsweek* as a civilized country with economic problems such as inflation, parliamentary debates, election campaigns, railway accidnts, and earthquakes.

Novoye Vremya (New Times)

When we go "through the looking-glass" we see a picture of the United States from the Soviet newsmagazine's point of view. The results of the content analysis of *Novoye Vremya* can be seen in Table 10.3.

It should be noted here that by 1989 the general thematic content of *Novoye Vremya* had undergone serious changes. From a weekly magazine of world affairs with scant coverage of Soviet interior issues, it turned into a more traditional newsmagazine in which the USSR's domestic affairs received more prominence at the expense of foreign news and features. Therefore, a

Table 10.3 *Novoye Vremya* American Stories

	1985	% of space	Cover Stories	1987	% of space	Cover Stories	1989	% of space	Cover Stories
	sq. in.			sq. in.			sq. in.		
Internal affairs	1,800	9.2	1	3,130	13.4	0	2,470	21.0	1
Foreign policy	11,170	57.0	3	7,680	32.8	0	5,320	45.2	0
Military issues	6,620	33.8	5	12,590	53.8	12	3,980	33.8	1
Total	19,580	100.0	9	23,400	100.0	12	11,770	100.0	2

decrease of the absolute figures in 1989 does not translate into any decrease of interest in U.S. affairs.

It is clear from the table that compared to 1985 a slight increase of space given to news and features about life inside the United States took place at the expense of reports concentrating on foreign affairs, with a stable proportion of military issues. A clearer picture emerges from Table 10.4.

Dealing with the domestic life of the United States, *Novoye Vremya* conjures up three different images of the country in three cases.

In 1985, it only allotted 9 percent of the total space to America, which was portrayed as a society where human rights were violated and the people suffered in the grips of Reaganomics and ecological problems.

In 1987, the main topic of the reports was "Irangate" and other political scandals. Coverage of human rights abuses was half as much as in 1985 and dealt mainly with a historical view on them: More was written about Dr. Martin Luther King than about Dr. Charles Hyder. The grip of Reaganomics was replaced with "the hangover of Reaganomics" (1987, No. 13).

More prominence was given to literature and art. Moreover, whereas in the first 11 issues of *Novoye Vremya* just one article on literature and art was published—a story on anti-Soviet movies and books in the U.S. (in 1985 there were two articles, on antiwar issues and anti-Soviet art)—in the next 15 issues there were six articles about various aspects of American culture, but *none* about anti-Soviet or antiwar art. Nevertheless we cannot say that the face of American capitalism, though it changed its expression, became attractive to the Soviet reader.

The most important changes in presenting reports about the United States occurred in 1989. A new heading—"Experience"—appeared. Different sides of American life—the way the Congress works, the conversion of the defense industries, copyright protection, methods of combating disaster effects, and others—were favorably discussed. The idea was how to apply the American experience to Soviet realities.

Table 10.4 *Novoye Vremya* American Story Topics

Topic	1985 sq. in.	1985 % of space	1987 sq. in.	1987 % of space	1989 sq. in.	1989 % of space
News and commentary about U.S. internal affairs	1,800	100	3,130	100	2,470	100
Political scandals	40	2.2	930	29.7	70	2.8
Disasters	30	1.7	—	0	—	0
Human rights	370	20.6	300	9.6	140	5.7
Experience and ideas	—	0	—	0	430	17.4
Science and technology	100	5.6	120	3.8	230	9.3
Culture and art	130	7.2	550	17.6	650	26.3
News and commentary on U.S. external affairs	11,170	100	7,680	100	5,320	100
U.S.-Soviet relations	1,900	17.0	1,870	24.3	3,300	62.0
-Historical aspects of the relations	1,760	15.8	1,030	13.4	910	17.1
"People's diplomacy"	100	.9	160	2.1	740	13.9
Covert actions, "state terrorism," CIA activities	2,630	23.5	1,230	16.0	280	5.3
Relations with Latin America, Canada	2,000	17.9	1,130	14.7	540	10.2
U.S. relations with Africa	920	8.2	190	2.5	140	2.6
U.S. and the Middle East, Gulf Region	640	5.7	540	7.0	—	0
U.S. and the Far East (Japan, China, Korea)	590	5.3	1,380	18.0	750	14.1
U.S. and Afghanistan, Pakistan, India	220	2.0	280	3.6	—	0
U.S. relations with Australia, New Zealand, Oceania	220	2.0	430	5.6	—	0
Bilateral relations with other countries	400	3.6	180	2.3	90	1.7

Human rights was a topic for just one report, about the necessity of parliamentarian cooperation in this field (1989, No. 26). More space was provided for the coverage of cultural life in America, but this was mainly attributable to the increased number of reports about "American Russians" such as artist Ernst Neizvestny.

The best way to show the transformation of the U.S. image in the pages of *Novoye Vremya* is to compare two covers devoted to the life of Americans. (There were only two such covers in the examined period.) On the cover of a 1985 issue we see a youngster at a crossroad with pointers reading "drug addiction," "unemployment," "crime," and "poverty." Above the black, green, and gray picture is the heading "U.S. Youth: Grim Problems, Gloomy Prospects" (1985, No. 26). Young Americans can also be seen on a 1989 cover, but here it is a multicolor photo with a view of the Statue of Liberty. The heading reads: "Room at the Top: How to Make Good in America" (1989, No. 2).

Political, social, and economic issues of U.S. foreign policy as covered by *Novoye Vremya* in 1985 came to various plots of the CIA, interference in the affairs of Third World countries, subversion of international organizations (UNESCO), "ecological terrorism" (Bhopal, etc.), and cooperation with the USSR during World War II. Such descriptions of aggressive policies with a tint of yearning for the bygone friendship could only strengthen the image of "enemy-traitor." The tone of *Novoye Vremya* reports fits the image. Consider a typical quotation:

> The United States and its monopolies plunder the Latin American continent. Their puppets—local rulers—plunder the peoples of the countries they govern. Such a situation suits both Washington, and its puppets—heads of reactionary regimes—perfectly. (*Novoye Vremya*, 1985, No. 3, p. 19)

In 1987 this image changed somewhat. When reporting world events, *Novoye Vremya* didn't mention U.S. "wrecking activities" in *every* item and gave less space to reports about U.S. state terrorism and CIA intrigue. The magazine published an interview with UN Ambassador Jeane Kirkpatrick (1987, No. 7), a rare honor for an American politician at that time. The report symbolized the possibility of a new and balanced approach to coverage of the international situation. Nevertheless, the tone of the *Novoye Vremya* stories remained the same: "The United States is resorting to dirty tricks to make the Ghanaians give up their fight for a better future" (*Novoye Vremya*, 1989, No. 11, p. 26).

The greatest changes in American-related content occurred in 1989 (as in the domestic information; see Table 10.3). References to the "American factor" appeared less and less often in reports about different countries. What used to be called "neocolonialism" became "a rather complicated relationship between the industrialized and developing nations" (*Novoye Vremya*, 1989, No. 26, p. 13). Most of the talk here was about Soviet-American relations and contact—and that went on when there were no summits or other dramatic changes in the bilateral relations!

A great deal of attention was paid to "peoples' diplomacy," that is, the movement of common people for mutual understanding and cooperation between the two countries.

Traditionally *Novoye Vremya* gives prominence to the problems of disarmament and world security. Special focus on these issues in 1987 is easily explained by the International Forum of Peace Forces held then in Moscow with a great deal of Soviet press attention. The tone of the reports in this topic became calmer in 1989. The "counter-propagandistic" charges or other labels, such as the following 1985 editorial illustrates, were no longer prevalent:

> They [the aggressive imperialist circles, above all those in the U.S.] have resurrected the Hitlerite myth of the "Soviet military threat." Goebbels-style lies have again gained currency. Suffice it to note the diplomatic and propaganda maneuvers over the "star wars" program. (*Novoye Vremya*, 1985, No. 20, p. 1)

In short, *Novoye Vremya* in 1989 gave the United States an image of a friendly nation from whom we could learn much. The absence of negative information about unemployment, abuses of human rights, and CIA activities adds idealistic features to the image. Pro-American enthusiasm compensates for the grim perception of the United States in days gone by. But it might bring about ill-grounded hopes for gratuitous assistance and various concessions to the Soviet Union. Then hopes will be replaced by disillusionment and disappointment.

In conclusion, both *Newsweek* and *Novoye Vremya* did a good job in transforming Soviet and American images on their pages. Although these images became somewhat idealistic, generally speaking the nature of the reports in 1989 was more serious and favorable. The main outcome was that enemy images were transformed into partner images.

11
Enemy, Friend, or Competitor?
A Content Analysis of the
Christian Science Monitor and *Izvestia*

MARIUS ALEKSAS LUKOSIUNAS

Is it possible to compare the mass media of the Soviet Union and the United States? The answer to this question serves as a brief introduction to this chapter, which analyzes a Soviet newspaper, *Izvestia,* and a U.S. newspaper, the *Christian Science Monitor.*

The main task of every mass medium in every country is to reflect and form public opinion and to help evaluate the perspective of the development of modern society. This basic task of the mass media at the same time is a central characteristic of a democratic society. There are no arguments against this conclusion either in Soviet scientists' works or in the works of their Western colleagues. Classic Western conceptions such as Siebert, Peterson, and Schramm's four theories of the press (which we may call a predecessor of many theoretical works), as well as the most orthodox works on the mass media in the USSR, for a long time denied real implementation of this characteristic in the mass media of their opponents. I believe that the decades of such theoretical opposition are over. Concepts, which are normative, tied to a concrete political and ideological situation, gave way to scientific analysis, which was for the first time formulated in the five-pronged question of Harold Lasswell: "Who says what, in which channel, to whom, with what effect?"

Any arguments that are against scientific analysis and opposed to its ideological evaluations are mired in the past. The vocabulary of the past in the Soviet Union used the term *class antagonism* in relation to the United States—that of an uncompromising struggle with totalitarianism. I think that the reality of the 1980s provides answers to the question of the possibility of comparing the mass media of the United States and the USSR positively.

In this chapter, I will analyze the reporting of the Soviet Union's domestic affairs in the pages of the *Christian Science Monitor* and the newspaper

Izvestia's representation of life in the United States for the periods from March through May of 1985 and 1989. This chronological framework was chosen for specific reasons. In March 1985 Mikhail Gorbachev was elected general secretary of the CPSU Central Committee. In May, during his visit to Leningrad, Gorbachev changed all stereotypes of communication between the power and the people, as a correspondent of *Newsweek* noted. In March, April, and May of 1989 the elections to the Congress of the People's Deputies were held and the work of a new Soviet parliament began.

The researchers of this study therefore analyzed how the mass media of the United States had reflected the development of the events in the USSR from the beginning of the destruction of the "people/power" stereotype to the formation of the structures that changed these relations in reality. We also tried to trace the changes in the attitude of *Izvestia* toward domestic affairs in the United States and track the ways in which these developments reflected the changes in the scale of values of Soviet society.

The analysis of domestic affairs gave us a chance to determine the information politics of the newspapers more deeply and precisely for several reasons:

(1) The reflection and evaluation of the processes taking place in another country demanded more active rejection of stereotypes.

(2) The political situation influenced the reflection of domestic affairs less than that of the foreign information.

(3) The information about domestic affairs was loosely tied to news agencies and other official or government bodies.

One could also conclude from these three points that journalists were able to show their autonomy and independence more often in reports on domestic affairs of another country.

The *Christian Science Monitor*

The newspaper from March to May 1985 printed 13 reports about domestic affairs in the Soviet Union. During the same months in 1989 there was a sharp increase to 37 reports (see Table 11.1).

From 1985 to 1989 the number of reports increased almost threefold. Editorial space for political, economic, and ethnic relations increased approximately to the same extent. There was also an increase in the reports about human rights, but interest in social relations and culture declined in 1989. The mass media of the world focused on perestroika and the processes of

Table 11.1

Coverage of USSR Domestic Affairs by the *Christian Science Monitor*

Topic	1985			1989		
	# of reports	sq. cm.	% of space	# of reports	sq. cm.	% of space
Politics	3	1,430	25.4	14	5,792	37.4
Economics	2	855	15.2	7	2,610	16.9
Social relations	2	606	10.7	1	400	2.6
Human rights	2	810	14.5	5	2,290	14.8
Ethnic	—	—	—	9	3,595	23.2
Culture	4	1,922	34.2	—	—	—
Ecology	—	—	—	1	800	5.1
Total	13	5,623	100.0	37	15,487	100.0

reform under way in the USSR, and the *Christian Science Monitor* was no exception. That is why in our analysis we compared absolute figures for 1985 and 1989 as well as relative percentages in every topical category in 1985 and 1989. Such an analysis gave us an opportunity not only to fix the increase or decrease of interest toward the Soviet Union but also to analyze the deeper structural changes in the informational policy of the newspaper.

Editorials that covered political relations made up 25.4 percent of the space in 1985 and 37.4 percent in 1989, an increase of 12 percentage points. The topic "ethnic relations" made the biggest jump, from no coverage in 1985 to 23.2 percent in 1989. Human rights, economics, and ecology topics increased somewhat for both time periods, while topics on culture and social relations declined. Such developments of informational politics illustrate that ethnic and political relations are now basic for the *Christian Science Monitor* to estimate the level of changes in the USSR.

Politics

In the report "The Russians Get New Czar to Revive Their Ailing Empire" (March 15, 1985), the writer made a point about continuity of monarchical Russia's politics in the Soviet Union. The author seemed doubtful that the country would overcome the crisis. Another report (March 3, 1985) concluded that without giving military programs up, it would be impossible to overcome the crisis. American journalists assumed that the right and ability to make political decisions belonged only to Mr. Gorbachev. He was compared with Peter the Great and Katherine the Second. The general secretary personified the only political force—the CPSU. Such an approach confirmed that the Soviet Union remained an authoritarian state, the *Christian Science Monitor* essentially concluded in 1985.

In March, April, and May 1989 we observed another picture. The number of stories increased by 11 reports and editorial space by four times. The dynamics of domestic political life and the struggle between old and new thinking in the CPSU was characterized by Paul Quinn-Judge, the *Christian Science Monitor* correspondent in Moscow, in "Gorbachev Balances" (April 25, 1989) and "Gorbachev Outwits the Opponents" (April 27, 1989). On May 2, Quinn-Judge's report read that the opponents were anti-liberals and anti-intellectuals. In the second part of the report an accurate political portrait of opponents was drawn with the help of Yegor Yakovlev, editor of *Moscow News,* and Nail Bikenin, editor of *Kommunist.* If in 1985 the possiblity of the reforms was evaluated pessimistically, in 1989 the reader could find two positions—conservative and reformist—on this issue, as well as different ways of solving the problem according to the reformers. Analyzing the stand of Boris Yeltsin (May 24, 1989), the correspondent told the readers that this political leader did not oppose Mr. Gorbachev. The second part of the report contradicted the conclusion because the correspondent wrote that several interviews that had appeared in the local press showed Yeltsin's ambivalent view of Gorbachev.

The information sources of the *Christian Science Monitor* over this period became more credible, whereas they once were gleaned from gossip, dissidents' opinions, or pointless speeches of Soviet leaders. In the later years information came from the local and alternative press, interviews with state officials, representatives of new political organizations, and scholars and writers with their independent views of the situation. The picture was more diverse, with one stable feature: There were no items by conservative-minded authors. We could only find opinions that either supported Mr. Gorbachev as he personified the reforms or were even more radical. Political labels remained in the newspaper only in regard to anti-liberals and anti-reformists.

Ethnic Relations

Ethnic issues "are the most serious problems which concern the present and future of Soviet politics," stated Sovietologist Adam Ulam (Voice of America, October 3, 1988). The *Christian Science Monitor* echoes Ulam's statement, with the biggest increase in space—23.2 percentage points. The April and May issues of the newspaper paid the greatest attention to the republic of Georgia. In the May 17 and 20 issues, the newspaper gave prominence to Mr. Gorbachev's attitude toward the situation. Paul Quinn-Judge, through the statements of his interlocutors, Andrei Sakharov and Yegor Yakovlev, expressed the opinion that the events in Georgia had been a provocation against Mikhail Gorbachev and the reformers. On May 5, the *Christian Science Monitor* stated that the "Lithuanian disaster" (that is, the total Communist party defeat in the elections to the Supreme Soviet) and the reports from Georgia confirmed that ethnic relations was the most complicated issue for the reformers.

On March 7 we saw a confirmation of the notion that the Baltic republics were a testing ground for the whole Soviet Union. But in an earlier story, Quinn-Judge evaluated the situation as troublesome when deputies from Sajudis, a grass-roots movement in Lithuania, announced in the newly elected republican parliament their decision to secede from the USSR, saying that the deputies would be "provoking a major and possibly fatal confrontation with Moscow" (May 5, 1989). That marked the first time the newspaper was not totally sympathetic to the opposition. As we saw before, the *Christian Science Monitor* did not support confrontation and radical steps by various nationalistic groups. However, on April 20, 1989, the *Monitor* stated in the opinion section that the essence of Mikhail Gorbachev's ethnic policy was to divide, isolate, and set on to fight different nations. This analysis confirmed that in May 1989 the *Christian Science Monitor* did not have a clear conception of how the processes of reforms in the ethnic sphere would develop.

Economics

In 1985 the *Monitor* reported the crisis in the Soviet economy. The newspaper doubted the possibility of starting reforms or implementing reformist programs with any success. In 1989 the number of reports and editorial space increased more than threefold. As a part of editorial space in 1989, however, economics coverage increased by only 1.7 percentage points. There were no doubts about the decision to reform the economy, but the cautious stand of the newspaper concerning quick results of the reform was demonstrated in a typical article in 1989 with the headline "Soviet Agriculture Still Has Tough Row to Hoe" (March 15, 1989).

Human Rights

The number of reports on human rights topics increased 1.5 times, from 2 in 1985 to 5 in 1989. But in both 1985 and 1989 editorial space remained virtually the same—14.5 percent and 14.8 percent. The changes of the newspaper's position can be illustrated by the following two examples. On March 6, 1985, a report said that human and religious rights were violated throughout the country. On April 15, 1989, Paul Quinn-Judge concluded that in the sphere of human rights "political changes are coming faster than anyone believes." The changes in the religious situation were reflected in an article written by Metropolitan Filaret. His stand was simple: "Many of our problems are correctly understood by our leadership" (April 3, 1989).

The transformation of stereotypes could be seen in the work of one journalist who wrote about human rights in the report "Underground Nun from Lithuania" (April 24, 1989). The hero of the story, Nijole Sadunaite, said: "Soviet power is basically Stalinist . . . beginning with Lenin and ending with Gorbachev." Only one argument—"Gorbachev and Stalin smile identically"—was used by Nijole Sadunaite to support her statement. The journalist, like most of his American colleagues, preferred not to express his opinion in order to observe the ritual of objectivity. But silence is also a position. The journalist didn't help Sadunaite find better or more rational arguments. The author could not have seriously believed that the smile had a major role in the political process, nor could he have thought the intellectual audience of the *Christian Science Monitor* would not perceive the negative connotation of the story. We understand the subjectivity of this evaluation and note that only a tendency to be guided by the formal criteria put this story into the negative group.

The last group of topics—reports about culture, social relations, and ecology—is reflected to such a small extent that it is impossible to draw any firm conclusions. Reports about culture and social relations both decreased from 1985 to 1989, while reports about ecology increased only slightly. The reason for the decrease could have been that serious items about ethnic conflicts and political relations took the place of art reviews and reports about the drinking habits of Russians.

The changes in topics did not clarify the position of the newspaper toward the processes that took place in the Soviet Union. Every report had its own evaluation of the events. Here we created three categories—positive, negative, and neutral—in which to characterize the attitude of the *Christian Science Monitor*.

Positive coverage reflected a positive or favorable attitude toward Soviet reforms, political, ethnic, and economic stability, and social cohesion. Negative coverage emphasized social conflicts, political, economical, and ethnic instability, and an unfavorable attitude toward Soviet reforms. Neutral coverage was balanced, fair, and unbiased reporting. One could argue that these categories are subjective. Stagnation could be transformed by a reporter into stability, and conflicts could be deemed steps to democracy rather than the

Table 11.2
Neutral, Positive, and Negative Coverage of the USSR in the *Christian Science Monitor*

Topic	1985			1989		
	# of reports	sq. cm.	% of space	# of reports	sq. cm.	% of space
Neutral	5	2,368	42	22	10,491	68
Positive	1	239	5	4	861	6
Negative	7	2,986	53	10	4,135	26
Total	13	5,593	100	36	15,487	100

disorganization of social life. That is why, in evaluating each report, we considered the following questions: What situation is conserved with the help of stability? In what direction is the conflict pushing society—backward to the times of dictatorship and confrontation, or forward to the future of fruitful development?

American scholars B. Blake and E. Haroldsen say that conflict is the most attractive value of a report to the reader. Presentation of conflict in the newspaper changed during the period studied. In 1985, conflict was shown as a permanent clash between two opposite systems. In 1989, conflict was portrayed as constructive competition between old and new thinking. One might object to our narration, saying that it is subjective. That is why we used standardized features to guide us in characterizing the reports. Nevertheless, we cannot pretend that this analysis is totally objective.

From Table 11.2 we can see that reports in the neutral category increased in every topic. Compared to 1985, the number of neutral stories and space in 1989 grew sharply by 4.4 times. Neutral items increased 3.4 times in 1989 in the amount of space. The number of positive items increased fourfold, and there was a 3.6 times increase in the amount of space. The percent of positive reports increased by only 1 percentage point. The number of negative reports and their space increased about 1.4 times in 1989. The total number of reports and space increased from 1985 to 1989 by 2.8 times. The number of neutral stories in 1989 reflected the *Monitor*'s desire to become more objective. But it is impossible to predict whether this trend will continue into the future. A dissemination of the categories in all topics except culture reflects the *Christian Science Monitor*'s tendency toward information politics—the increase of neutral information and the decrease of negative information. Positive information increased only slightly, with one exception—a 30 percent increase in the human rights category. This exception could be

Table 11.3
Coverage of U.S. Domestic Affairs by *Izvestia*

Topic	1985			1989		
	# of reports	sq. cm.	% of space	# of reports	sq. cm.	% of space
Politics	10	1,638	17.5	3	1,540	20.2
Economics	5	1,699	18.1	1	160	2.0
Social relations	6	1,199	12.8	2	520	6.8
Human rights	16	3,120	33.4	—	—	—
Crime	3	390	4.2	6	770	10.1
Culture	5	1,301	14.0	13	4,645	60.9
Total	45	9,347	100.0	25	7,635	100.0

explained as the recognition of the Soviet achievements in this field. Another exception to the general trends is a 31 percent increase in negative information in the ethnic category. This figure accurately reflects the situation developing in the Soviet Union. On the whole, positive information in 1989 increased by about 3 times, negative information by 1.4 times, and neutral information by 4.4 times.

Izvestia

Eleven million copies of *Izvestia* are distributed daily, with 30 million people reading it. In 1989 the number of editorial reports covering the domestic affairs of the United States decreased 20 percentage points from the year 1985.

As shown in Table 11.3, the number of reports concerned with economics, social relations, and human rights decreased. Compared to 1985, editorial reports on these topics in 1989 decreased by 16.1, 6, and 33.4 percentage points, respectively.

What are the explanations for the declines in these areas? First of all, in 1985 there was a more critical attitude toward American society. In 1989 the USSR was faced with some serious problems of its own in the above-mentioned categories and the crises had still not been overcome, which is why the newspaper did not call its readers' attention to these topics. The paper thereby reaffirmed the conclusion of American social scientists that one of the objective functions of mass media is to serve as an instrument of social control to help keep stability in society. The second reason for the decrease in editorial space devoted to economics, social relations, and human rights is the stable development of these topics in American society. The third reason concerns the changes not only in Soviet ideology but also in the practice of journalism.

These changes can be illustrated by *Izvestia*'s characterizations of American entrepreneur Ted Turner, owner of Cable News Network. On May 4, 1985, the newspaper wrote that "the right-winger Ted Turner wants to buy CBS, Inc." On May 15, Turner was named "an aggressive, conservative businessman." By 1989 he had become one of the Soviet Union's best friends and was no longer called right-wing or aggressive. It is also impossible to imagine reports about American husbands beating their wives (March 7, 1985), appearing in *Izvestia* in 1989.

We noticed changes and decreases of stereotypes concerning human rights problems in the United States. In 1985, 75 percent of *Izvestia*'s reports were devoted to the problem of racism. In 1989 the problem, as well as the word *racism,* disappeared from its pages.

The coverage of political relations also changed. In 1985 newspapers presented the United States as a semifascist state. Forty percent of the reports and more than half of the editorial space were devoted to the increasing influence of fascism in the country. In 1989 the main political reports concerned the work of Congress, the Supreme Court, and other political institutions and the relations between the government and the citizens. The reports attempted to convey a positive image of American society to Soviet citizens. The reason for the increase of the reports and editorial space devoted to crime in 1989 was the Oliver North trial. Of course it must be noted that this political scandal was covered with the help of the Western mass media. Four reports devoted to this issue were reprinted from such sources as Reuters, UPI, and *Newsweek.*

Culture was the only topic that showed an increase in both the number of reports and the amount of editorial space. This topic contained not only reports about Hemingway or art reviews but also articles about the "congress of twins" and reports about the friendship between American and Soviet veterans of World War II. The Soviet-American alliance in World War II was the only subject covered positively in 1985.

Separate analysis of the editorial space in every category in 1985 and 1989 revealed that neutral coverage increased 78 percentage points, positive coverage increased by 7 points, and negative coverage decreased by 85 percentage points. Similar tendencies could be observed in comparing the number of reports in 1985 and 1989. Comparing these figures with Table 11.2, we see that the trends are similar in the increase of the neutral and the decrease of the negative categories.

Table 11.4
Neutral, Positive, and Negative Coverage of the United States in *Izvestia*

Topic	1985			1989		
	# of reports	sq. cm.	% of space	# of reports	sq. cm.	% of space
Neutral	4	338	4	22	6,328	82
Positive	3	819	9	2	1,160	16
Negative	38	8,189	87	1	147	2
Total	45	9,347	100	25	7,635	100

The increase and decrease in Table 11.2 are not so sharp as in Table 11.4 (26 percentage points and 27 points compared to 78 percentage points and 85 points in Table 11.4). The neutral coverage in 1989 occupied more than two thirds of the editorial space of *Izvestia,* which was very similar to the *Christian Science Monitor.* This fact confirmed that the rules of selection and evaluation of facts in the editorial offices were becoming more alike.

Conclusions

The coverage of domestic affairs of both the Soviet Union and the United States underwent tremendous changes in the years studied. In 1989 the *Christian Science Monitor* wrote more about the USSR than *Izvestia* reported about the United States. This is mainly because information about the Soviet Union has recently become the number one topic for the Western mass media.

The style of coverage by both American and Soviet journalists is becoming more similar, and the neutral category is becoming the dominant one. But the dynamics of this process are not the same. The *Izvestia* editorial policy changed more radically. On the one hand, the truth about domestic affairs in the United States is seen through rose-colored glasses. Yet on the basis of the ideals embodied in different aspects of U.S. social life (which are being propagandized by *Izvestia*), the newspaper is forming the necessary model of a possible interior structure for the Soviet Union. To form a public ideal is a priority for *Izvestia,* in our opinion.

In 1989, the reporting in the *Monitor* also was dominated by the neutral category. Reflection of the events, rather than the formation of a public ideal, was the priority for the American newspaper. It is possible to form a general conclusion that the two newspapers in 1989 rejected the extremes and became closer in style and rhetoric but remained different in their understanding of the functions of the mass media. These differences no longer lower journalism to the level of confrontation. That is why such quantitative changes are the guarantees of rapprochement. The *Christian Science Monitor* and *Izvestia* now look at each other with mutual concern and goodwill instead of suspicion and fear.

12
The Image of the Soviet Union
in Chinese Mass Media

XU YAOKUI

The mass media, including newspapers, magazines, radio, and televison, have become an integral part of China's daily life and its perception of the external world, as well as a means of international communication and international information. Our people learn and understand foreign nations mainly by way of mass media.

China is a socialist country led by the Communist party. All of its mass media work in accordance with the policy of the party. In other words, newspapers, magazines, radio, and television serve as instruments of propaganda for the party and the government's political aims. Media serve the interests of the whole of the people.

In my view, there were three periods in the development of Sino-Soviet relations. The first one started on October 1, 1949, the birthday of the new China, and ended approximately in the late 1950s. That was the best period of relations between China and the Soviet Union, characterized by close cooperation between the two countries. The nascent People's Republic of China (PRC) did its best to learn from the Soviet Union in as many areas as possible—from the political system and management of the economy to culture and public education. We translated nearly all Soviet books into Chinese. Soviet books and movies dominated our cultural life. Nearly every Chinese person, young and old, knew the name of Pavel Korchagin and sang such songs as "Oh, the snow-ball-tree blossoms . . . ," "Katyusha," and "Moscow Nights."

The Chinese people learned about the Soviet Union and its people mainly through books, newspapers, and movies. During this time the Soviet Union seemed to be, in the view of the Chinese, a great socialist country that headed a socialist network—a country that, after the defeat of German fascism in World War II, opposed American imperialism and defended peace in the world. This was the first image portrayed of the Soviet Union in the mass media of our country.

The Soviet Union was considered a model socialist state, and China eagerly imitated the Soviet Union without taking its own local circumstances into consideration. China saw the Soviet Union as a benevolent big brother. In fact, the only aid given to China at that time was from the Soviet Union and other socialist countries, who offered zealous and unselfish assistance to China in socialist construction.

That period, however, did not last for long. After only 10 years a more unpleasant era in Sino-Soviet relations began. This second stage ran from the early 1960s through the early 1980s and represented the lowest point in relations between China and the Soviet Union—nearly a complete break. During that time, the Soviet leadership ordered the withdrawal of all Soviet experts from China, an action that not only harmed China's economy and socialist construction, but also greatly offended the Chinese people.

The outbreak of the so-called Cultural Revolution caused even greater damage to the relations between the two countries. It was during the Cultural Revolution that the fight against revisionism, with the USSR serving as an example, spread throughout the country. Soviet military intervention in Czechoslovakian affairs in the 1960s and Afghan affairs in the 1970s complicated the bilateral relations even more. During that time, the Chinese people learned only about negative aspects of Soviet life from the mass media, as the Chinese journalists interpreted events in the Soviet Union from a critical and reproachful perspective. The media did not focus on any of the Soviet achievements or successes in science, culture, or sports. At that stage, in the eyes of China, the Soviet Union was a representative of modern revisionism conducting social-imperialistic foreign policy. There were virtually no ties between the two peoples.

A lessening of the tensions in Sino-Soviet relations became apparent in the beginning of the 1980s. When Mikhail Gorbachev became general secretary of the CPSU Central Committee, a new period of normalization in bilateral relations started. This occurred as a result of the defeat of the "Gang of Four" (a group blamed for many of the excesses of the Cultural Revolution), who had conducted an ultraleftist domestic and foreign policy. After the defeat of the Gang of Four, and especially after the third plenary meeting of the 11th convocation of the Communist Party of China Central Committee, our party chose the development of the national economy as the foundation of its work, putting forward the policy of "reform and doors open to the external world."

China and the Soviet Union developed many commonalities, especially with respect to political policies. Gorvachev had also implemented a new political policy of perestroika and glasnost in accordance with the new thinking, a turning point in the cooperation between the two countries. Gorbachev's visit to Beijing in May 1989 marked a normalization in the relations between China and the Soviet Union, and a new page in Sino-Soviet relations had turned.

Since the beginning of the 1980s, the Chinese media have interpreted Soviet life guided by principles of objectivity, truth, fairness, and noninterference with the internal affairs of other countries. As a result, the Chinese people have had an opportunity to see an accurate picture of the Soviet Union. Now the Chinese know that the Soviets still maintain their socialist state and have a friendly attitude toward their neighbor.

Below are the results of research I conducted to answer two questions: How do the Chinese mass media reflect present events in the Soviet Union? What are the Chinese readers, listeners, and TV viewers interested in? I analyzed the popular daily newspaper *Renmin ribau* (*People's Daily*) and programs of Central Television of China in May 1989. *Renmin ribau,* an official organ of the CPC Central Committee, is the most important and authoritative newspaper in China, with a daily circulation of about five million. It has eight large pages, with the most important information on domestic and foreign affairs printed on page 1. Domestic, political, economic, cultural, sports, and other issues are covered on pages 2, 4, 5, and 6, whereas pages 3 and 7 are reserved exclusively for international information and world problems. Page 8 is a literary and art supplement.

May 1989 was full of events and information in China. A wave of student demonstrations that began in April turned into disturbances throughout the month of May, becoming a focal point for Chinese newspapers, radio, and TV. May was also the month Gorbachev traveled to Beijing for the Sino-Soviet summit, another target of attention for Chinese journalists and the public.

These events each influenced the number of Soviet-related items in the Chinese newspapers in a different way. Because of the number of reports on the student disturbances, there may have been fewer items about the Soviet Union. However, Gorbachev's visit probably helped to increase the number of Soviet-related items. When reading the results of the following analysis one should keep these influences in mind (see Tables 12.1-12.3).

First, from previous studies in 1987 and 1988 we know that the number of Soviet-related items in May 1989 greatly increased in comparison. In May 1988 the number of Soviet-related items was 85, whereas in May 1987 there were 62. In other words, by May 1989 the number of such items had increased 41 percent compared with May 1988, and 94 percent compared with May

Table 12.1 Coverage of the USSR in the *People's Daily*

	Total number of items
News	89
Features	18
Pictures	13
Total	120

NOTE: News about Soviet sporting events printed in the sports section of the newspaper were not included in the table.

Table 12.2 Content of the *People's Daily* Items

Topics	Number
Sino-Soviet relations	32
Political life in the Soviet Union	30
Social problems in the Soviet Union	18
Military affairs	18
Literature and culture	10
Economics	8
Personalities	4

Table 12.3 Distribution of *People's Daily* Items Among Different Pages

Page	Number of Items	Percent
1	15	14.1
2	8	7.5
3	67	62.6
4	3	2.8
7	9	8.4
8	5	4.6
Total	107*	100.0

*Pictures not included.

1987. Second, journalists' attitudes toward the Soviet Union changed greatly. Whereas they had in the past reported about the Soviet Union from a critical point of view, by May 1989 their reports were much more objective and balanced.

Television. There are two television stations in Beijing: Chinese Central Television and Beijing Television, the latter broadcasting to Beijing and its suburbs only. Central TV has three channels. Channel 1 is a political information channel, as well as an arts and literature channel, for the entire country. Channel 2 is for economic and arts information, also broadcast nationwide. Channel 3 is exclusively an arts channel for Beijing citizens. Beijing TV also has three channels. Channel 1 is a political, literature, and arts information channel. Channel 2 is purely for arts information, and Channel 3 is for education.

Television is popular with the Chinese, with more than 100 million TV sets in the country. Every night more than 600 million Chinese watch TV. In May 1989 several TV programs about the USSR, such as "Moscow," "Soviet Union Today," "Byelorussian Circus and Folk Dances," and others were shown to the Chinese audience. In addition, Beijing TV broadcast the Soviet serial "Eternal Call" every day after May 15th.

In 1989, Chinese television journalists visited the Soviet Union to shoot a documentary entitled "Journey Down the Volga," which consisted of 31 segments. Beginning April 24, Central TV broadcast this serial, presenting a 10-minute film each day for an entire month. The documentary was of great interest to viewers because of its richness and visually pleasant footage. The serial, presenting images of Soviet people, their daily lives, and their customs, deeply impressed Chinese viewers. To summarize:

(1) Chinese journalists take care to inform their public about the Soviet Union in a truthful, fair, and timely manner. In conjunction with the improvement in Sino-Soviet relations, Soviet-related information occupies a more important place and gets more space in the mass media of China. This is shown by the increasing amount of attention paid by the government and people of China to the improvement of relations between the two nations and the two peoples.

(2) In the development of Sino-Soviet relations, mass media play an important role and serve as a window through which the Chinese people learn Soviet realities and understand the Soviet people, their work, and their lives.

(3) In general, mass media today play an important role in the lessening of international tensions, in mutual understanding, and in promoting friendship and cooperation among different countries and peoples.

13
The Image of the United States in Present-Day China

LIU LIQUN

The image of a country created by another country's media is significant in that the mass media bear the responsibility of portraying an accurate and balanced picture of a foreign country for their own people. Only in this way can the mass media serve as bridges to promote understanding between peoples and hence contribute to the friendship, peace, and social developments of the world. In this chapter I will analyze briefly the contents of a Chinese newspaper, the *People's Daily,* for the purpose of assessing the image of the United States in present-day China.

The *People's Daily* is in some sense a *Pravda* in China, an official organ of the Chinese Communist party (CCP) and a typical, representative, and authoritative newspaper. I sampled three complete monthly volumes of the paper for the month of May in 1987, 1988, and 1989 to see what kind of images the newspaper presented of the United States. In addition to the analysis of the *People's Daily,* I will touch on other major Chinese media in order to supply as much information as possible for the reader to form a clear picture of his or her own.

A Relatively Favorable Picture

Sino-American relations went through a very tense and hostile period after the end of the civil war in China with the victory of the CCP over the Kuomindang in 1949. After the United States and China established normal diplomatic relations in 1979, the relations between the two countries changed greatly. Since then, the Chinese media have not only increased their coverage of the United States, but they have also become more objective and even favorable in their coverage. In the *People's Daily* the number of foreign news items was 960, 1,029, and 756, respectively (see Table 13.1).

116

Table 13.1
Foreign News in the *People's Daily*

Country	May 1987		May 1988		May 1989		Total	
	# of items	(%)	# of items	(%)	# of items	(%)	# of items	(%)
U.S.-related news	129	(13.4)	162	(15.7)	120	(15.9)	411	(15.0)
Soviet-related news	78	(8.1)	96	(9.3)	83	(11.0)	257	(9.3)
Other foreign news	753	(78.4)	771	(74.9)	553	(73.1)	2,077	(75.7)
Total	960	(100)	1,029	(100)	756	(100)	2,745	(100)

Although the raw number of U.S.-related news items from 1988 to 1989 decreased, the percentage of total news increased over all three years from 13.4 to 15.7 and 15.9 percent. One obvious reason for the decrease in the number of foreign news items from 960 in 1987 to 756 in 1989, with a drop not only in U.S.-related news but in other foreign news as well, was that beginning in February of 1989, the *People's Daily* introduced a new layout design, reducing the previous two pages of foreign news to one and one-half pages to cut off unnecessary foreign news items and make room for advertisements or in-depth foreign reporting. In addition, May 1989 was an unusual month because of the Beijing students' demonstration and hunger strike followed by the imposition of martial law in some districts of Beijing by the Chinese government. I was told by the editors at the international department of the *People's Daily* that May of 1989 was not a typical month; there should have been more U.S.-related news items than there actually were.

May of 1989 should have been an inopportune time for presenting U.S.-related news and a particularly good time for presenting Soviet-related news because of the Sino-Soviet summit in Beijing, ending an abnormal diplomatic period of 30 years between the two countries. Nevertheless, the table shows 120 U.S.-related news items compared to only 83 Soviet-related reports.

More important, the quality of the coverage of the United States by the *People's Daily* improved with the increase in quantity. The paper tried to portray a balanced and sometimes favorable picture of the United States to the Chinese public. On May 2, 1988, the *Daily* presented a sentimental article titled "I Had Loved China Long Before Many Other Americans Did," quoting Shirley Temple. To accompany this article, the *Daily*'s editors ran another feature item on the same page entitled "Running for President and Competing for Office," which satirized the political campaign process in America. The same editorial policy prevailed on May 2, 1989: A report from New York

City described the splendid celebration marking the bicentennial anniversary of the United States Constitution, and on the same page a dispatch from Washington, DC, revealed the confrontation between the Pentagon and the White House over the assessment of perestroika in the Soviet Union.

An article titled "A Talk with 10 American Heroic Kids" was carried on the front page of the *People's Daily* on May 8, 1988, and put in a column called "Forum of the Week." The piece praised the heroic deeds of 10 youngsters, including a boy who had dived into a frozen pond to rescue another and one who saved a friend's life by giving artificial respiration. The paper called on its readers to select 10 similarly heroic Chinese youths to promote spiritual cultivation among the Chinese young people. For once the privileged party organ devoted the important front-page space in the "Forum of the Week" column to present American heroism to China. This would have been unimaginable 11 years ago.

A New Propaganda Wave

After about 11 years of relative tranquility and harmony with only occasional friction in Sino-American relations, a new unpleasant period is surfacing between the two countries, characterized partly by the Chinese press's new propaganda campaign to criticize the United States for "rude interference with internal affairs of China." This propaganda has certainly created a negative image of the United States, but its effects have yet to be evaluated.

The campaign began on May 13, when the *People's Daily* published a news report criticizing for the first time the Voice of America (VOA) for broadcasting an "utterly groundless" report claiming that Gorbachev was willing to speak at a university in Beijing but his request had been rejected by the Chinese government. Since then, shock waves have been extending to other targets with heavier attacks. The main charge against VOA was "rumor mongering" during the student unrest and later "the counterrevolutionary rebellion" in Beijing.

In June and July of 1989 many articles in the *People's Daily* strongly criticized VOA and other American media, such as AP and UPI. On June 12, the *People's Daily* reprinted an article from the *Beijing Daily,* "The Inglorious Action of the VOA." On July 9 it published "The Performance of VOA and its 'Peaceful Evolution' Strategy," and on June 21 an article titled "Denunciation of a Distorted Report from AP" appeared. At the same time, several American correspondents stationed in Beijing, including VOA's Beijing bureau chief Alan Pessin, were expelled from China by government authorities.

What is "peaceful evolution," then? This is a typical Cold War term that probably originated with former U.S. Secretary of State John Foster Dulles, who hoped that the third or fourth generations of the communist countries would be so influenced by the West that they would accept the capitalist system peacefully, with no need for military intervention from the outside. The term "peaceful evolution" had disappeared from the Chinese press for a long time but has recently been revived, perhaps an indication that the shadow of the Cold War is still lingering.

Following the campaign against American media such as VOA, the waves of the propaganda campaign spread to such issues as the illegal asylum given by the American embassy in Beijing to the Chinese dissidents Fang Lizhi and his wife He Shuxian, the U.S. government's economic sanctions against China, student demonstrations in the 1960s, and so on. In this respect, the *People's Daily* published a number of articles, with headlines such as "See How American Government Suppressed Mass Demonstrations" (June 30) and "See How the U.S. Government Trampled Human Rights" (July 7).

Another feature of this propaganda campaign was to show old films, especially war stories, on television. The main theme that the officials wanted viewers to pick up from these films was that the only saviors of China were the CCP and the socialist system. One of the most popular films shown on Chinese TV recently was *The Battle of Sangkuorung*. Over the past 40 years this film has played a role in shaping a negative image of the United States, and almost every Chinese citizen on the mainland remembers the film's theme song, "My Motherland," which ends with the words, "If friends come, we have good wine; but we also have hunting guns if the enemy comes." The "enemy" is, of course, a reference to the "American aggressors."

One of the main purposes of the propaganda campaign, besides reiterating the necessity to adhere to the four cardinal principles (CCP leadership, the socialist road, the people's democratic dictatorship, and Marxism-Leninism and Mao Zedong thought) and to fight against bourgeois liberalization, is to make clear to the Chinese public that VOA is an organ of the U.S. government; that the U.S. government is the representative of the American capitalist class; and that the United States is ever and always on the track of capitalism. According to this campaign, in the final analysis there is no essential change, no so-called goodwill from the U.S. Be careful not to be cheated. Beware of being lured.

This campaign did have some impact on a large portion of the older generation in China. The articles in the press and the films on TV reminded them of some painful memories in their own lives. The older generation could never forget the Sino-American Cooperative Organization (SACO) set up in

1941, which trained secret agents for the Kuomindang government to arrest and kill progressive underground activists before the new China was founded. Nor could they forget that the American navy and air force had transported a huge number of arms to the Kuomindang troops during the civil war to fight the Communist-led liberation army and guerrilla forces, and that after the CCP had won the final victory, American vessels and aircraft carriers cruised in the Taiwan Strait to impose the containment strategy.

But to the young people in China, the propaganda campaign's effects were not clear, and scientific surveys were necessary. The attitude of the Chinese young people toward VOA may serve as an indicator of their response to the official media in China. During the students' unrest and later the "counter-revolutionary rebellion," it was reported that radio sets with shortwave bands had been completely sold out in shops and that the salesclerks were telling the customers how to find VOA frequencies. In addition, people in Beijing would go to loudspeakers on university campuses, on buildings by the streets, and in Tiananmen Square to broadcast tape recordings from VOA's Chinese service. These loudspeakers and recordings were installed and taped mostly by the young people.

A Soviet correspondent said, "If the people hear something on VOA that is not in the official Soviet press, they are going to say to themselves that the party has something to hide, and if they are hiding something from us, then we probably have to trust what VOA or the BBC is saying." It was and still is believed that the young people in China, especially the university students, do trust the VOA, just as the Soviet correspondent described.

What is the U.S. image in the eyes of the Chinese younger generation now? What effects has the new propaganda campaign had on those young people? The long queues of young students outside the TOEFL offices (Test of English as a Foreign Language) in Beijing, trying to register for this test in order to go to the United States, answer the above questions without much difficulty.

Open-Door Policy and Image Creating

The CCP's policy of opening to the outside world has also been playing a very important role in helping the Chinese public form images of foreign countries over the last 11 years, regardless of the foreign country. This policy was formally approved and adopted by the CCP and the Chinese government in 1978, when the third plenary session of the 11th CCP Congress was held in Beijing as a milestone marking the beginning of a new era in Chinese history. If we believe that the mass media are powerful instruments for influencing opinions and creating images and that over the last 11 years the Chinese media have portrayed a more accurate, balanced, or even favorable picture of the United States to the Chinese audience, then we should also realize that the Chinese media are both dominated and benefited by China's open-door policy. If we consider the structure of mass media as a kind of communication channel between China and the United States, we should remember that it was born from this open-door policy. It was this policy that helped China establish communication channels with the United States in addition to news reports, including economic, cultural, educational, scientific, diplomatic, military, and tourist exchanges. These exchanges have helped bring colorful, three-dimensional images of the United States to the Chinese people. The cultural exchange, for example, especially the introduction of U.S. pop culture and its images to the Chinese audience, has had a penetrating and magical effect.

Since the Chinese government finally won its position in the United Nations, it has developed more flexible policies in world affairs, including the Taiwan issue. And because the U.S. government eventually gave up its containment policy toward new China and sought to improve relations between the two countries, the so-called "iron curtain" or "bamboo curtain" was lifted.

There is an old Chinese saying: "It is easier to draw a picture of a ghost than a man." This is because nobody knows what a ghost really looks like. The same is true with image creation. When information obstacles or news blockades exist, people tend to form the image of an alien country by imagination based on false information; therefore, they often draw an inaccurate picture. When the obstacles are removed, people's eyes are opened. They have more access to information, which helps them get rid of the old, inaccurate, or stereotyped pictures in their minds and draw new ones. But a new problem emerges: How can people draw correct and accurate pictures of an object when they have not only their own information but also their own value judgments?

To draw a picture of an object with which one is somewhat acquainted can be difficult or controversial. There is another Chinese saying that follows the one above: "The benevolent see benevolence and the wise see wisdom," meaning that different people have different views of the same object. This probably has something to do with people's individual aesthetic values, but it is true of the image of the United States in China today. The younger generation tends to see the United States as a rich, modern, open, and democratic country with hardworking, independent, open-minded, carefree, and easygoing people. But the older generation certainly is not able to see the United States as its children do, and sometimes the two generations have fierce arguments.

One recent example is their sharply different attitudes toward the "Goddess of Democracy" on Tiananmen Square, erected just a few days before the military crackdown on the Beijing rebellion. The younger generation generally saw the Goddess of Democracy as a noble and beautiful statue, a symbol of progressiveness worthy of their admiration and love. In contrast, the older generation saw the Goddess as eccentric and ugly, a symbol of a hypocritical capitalist society in the West that deserved nothing but hatred.

One may wonder if the open-door policy will be stopped or changed after the crackdown and if the information blockade between China and the United States will be set up again. Soon after the martial-law troops occupied Tiananmen Square, the Chinese government proclaimed that China would never change its open-door policy. Of course we can see that this policy was and still is functioning in some way. For example, American pop culture is so pervasive in China that people cannot help but form their images of the United States under its influence. Watching Chinese TV news reports carefully in 1989, one could have observed a burned conversation handbook for traveling in the United States on the ground at Tiananmen Square near a students' canvas tent. One could also see that after the armored personnel vehicles crushed the Goddess of Democracy, the martial-law troops were praised and treated with cans of Coca-Cola. One scene showed some soldiers celebrating their victory by disco dancing and break dancing in their camps. Bold foreign travelers might have found this interesting scene: a line of military trucks and armed soldiers on duty in front of a Kentucky Fried Chicken restaurant in Beijing. It was said that for some time one of these restaurants in Beijing provided martial-law soldiers with 2,000 buckets of Kentucky Fried Chicken every day. The irony can be clearly seen.

American TV series are still being shown. The radio language-teaching programs are also still being broadcast. During the Cultural Revolution, learning or teaching English was regarded as something bourgeois or even taboo. Today martial law in Beijing has not done anything to stop the teaching of English on radio or TV. After June 3, 1989, when the martial-law troops at last fired at the "ruffians," amid the vigorous propaganda campaign against bourgeois liberalization, the "English on Sundays" program on the Chinese Central Broadcasting Station continued presenting talks in English. During June and July, this station gave seven talks in nine weeks on American life and society.

Is the Cold War Over?

When we discuss the image of the United States in present-day China, we might also consider the question: Is the U.S. still our enemy or is the Cold War over? This question probably causes more concern today among people in the Soviet Union and the United States than in China. This issue warrants closer examination because it is closely related to image creating and because people in both the East and the West have never been as anxious to put an end to the Cold War as they are today.

The Cold War generally refers to the tension after World War II between the Eastern socialist countries headed by the Soviet Union and the Western capitalist countries headed by the United States. But China today, although it still adheres to socialism and Marxism as its ideological foundation, has not been allied with the Eastern bloc since the 1960s, nor has it been allied with the Western countries. China today is a nonaligned country with an independent foreign policy that has established normal diplomatic relations with the United States in the West and has resumed its normal relations with the Soviet Union in the East. Different degrees of tension did exist at times not only between China and the United States but also between China and the Soviet Union, as in the 1960s. More important is the return of harmony. These facts may serve as evidence that China is playing a special independent role in world affairs today, thus keeping away from the Cold War.

Generally speaking, the tension between China and the United States has eased greatly since the Shanghai communiqué was signed by the two countries in 1972. Since then, China has hosted five consecutive U.S. presidents: Richard Nixon, Gerald Ford, Jimmy Carter, Ronald Reagan, and George Bush, with Bush experiencing unprecedented treatment as a climax in the two countries' harmonious relationship. American warships are no longer seen cruising the Taiwan Strait, the once-major hot spot, nor is there any artillery shelling by the People's Liberation Army over small islands occupied by the Kuomindang forces. The Chinese people no longer view the Americans as "American imperialists," "American devils," or "American aggressors," but as American professors, experts, visitors, or, in general, "American friends." We can definitely claim that the Cold War is over between China and the United States.

But if we narrow the original definition of the Cold War to a propaganda war between the two countries, we can sniff the smoke of gunpowder in newspapers and magazines, on TV screens, or from the radio announcers. Now the smell of the propaganda war is becoming even stronger than before.

Ever since he started the current economic reform in China, Chinese leader Deng Xiaoping has been calling on all members of the CCP and the Chinese people to wage relentlessly the resolute struggle against bourgeois liberalization in China.

After the crackdown of the counterrevolutionary rebellion in Beijing, numerous articles were published in official media to criticize "bourgeois freedom," "bourgeois democracy," and "so-called human rights," as well as the system of separation of powers and checks and balances in the United States. In the meantime, the American media have also devoted an unprecedented amount of space, time, and energy to attacking "communist totalitarianism," "communist dictatorship," and the violation of human rights in China. The propaganda war is still fierce and poignant and by no means over. The crusades against ideological enemies on both sides are proceeding with the force of military battles.

Conclusion

So complex is the image of the United States in China today that I can only present a brief look at it. What have we seen and what impressions have been formed in our minds so far?

(1) Since normalization of diplomatic relations between China and the United States in 1979, the Chinese media, with the *People's Daily* as a typical example, have portrayed a relatively accurate, balanced, and often favorable picture of the United States to the Chinese audience.

(2) Right before and after the putting down of the Beijing counterrevolutionary rebellion, the Chinese official media launched a heavy propaganda campaign to refute the American news media's accusations against the Chinese government and to bring back the old unfavorable images of the United States to the Chinese public. This campaign has had some impact on the older generation, but its effect on the younger generation has yet to be examined.

(3) The open-door policy adopted by the Chinese government has brought about not only news exchanges between China and the United States, but also many other channels of communication including economic, educational, cultural, scientific, diplomatic, tourist, and even military exchanges. Among them, the pop culture of the United States has played a very penetrating and even magic role in creating the image of the United States in China. The Chinese government reiterated after the crackdown on the Beijing rebellion that its open-door policy would not be changed. As a result, although the propaganda campaign is going on, the Chinese media continue to present articles and programs introducing American culture and American values.

(4) As China is now an independent and nonaligned socialist country, it is no longer involved in the Cold War. The tension between China and the United States has definitely been eased. The Chinese people no longer see the United States as an enemy but as a friend. However, the propaganda war is not over but revived, and the crusades against ideological enemies will continue for a long time.

In short, harmony and tension coexist now between China and the United States. If the governments of both countries realize that it was not easy for us to have become friends and continue to stress the need for dialogue, and if the mass media of both countries endeavor to present balanced, accurate, and multifaceted pictures of each other, they will be contributing not only to the mutual understanding of our two countries but to ending the Cold War in the world as well.

14
The End of the Cold War and the Opportunities for Journalism

DONNA EBERWINE
ROBERT KARL MANOFF
R. MICHAEL SCHIFFER

For Americans and indeed the world one of the most striking images of the past decade was that of young Germans dancing atop the Berlin Wall as it was breached, practicing a primitive form of détente from below. More powerfully than any arms control or human rights agreements could, such unlikely images have recently conveyed the fact that international relations are now being revolutionized.

The perception that something truly epochal is at hand is shared by policymakers and the public alike. A recent public opinion survey found that 72 percent of Americans believe that "things in the Soviet Union have changed fundamentally and we will probably see a new relationship between the two countries." Only 21 percent said they believed that a "return to the old ways" was likely.

The American media, after a period of initial skepticism, began to take their own measure of this revolutionary moment in early 1989. In a series of op-ed pieces, *The New York Times* invited experts in international relations and Soviet politics to address the question, "Is the Cold War over?" In its May 15, 1989, issue, *Newsweek* published a special report, "After the Cold War," examining the emerging U.S.-Soviet relationship. Its more conservative counterpart, *U.S. News & World Report,* devoted three special sections to examining the changes in the Soviet Union under the leadership of General Secretary Gorbachev and their impact on U.S. foreign policy. A leading newspaper chain, Knight-Ridder, published a five-part series on "The Challenge of Peace" in the post-Cold War era for America and for the world. Thanks to the media, "Is the Cold War over?" was becoming a common question well before the Malta summit took place and the Bush administration helped supply an answer in the affirmative.

126

It was in this context that the Center for War, Peace, and the News Media decided to turn the tables on journalists, posing the question the media had been asking of policymakers directly to the reporters themselves. What do journalists—who report these changes and analyze their import—think about whether the Cold War is over, we wanted to know. More importantly, what do they think these momentous changes mean for the practice of their own profession? In their roles as observers, reporters, and analysts, these members of the fourth estate are key players in the changing East-West environment. It was in fact a journalist, Herbert Swope, who first coined the term Cold War, and another, Walter Lippmann, who popularized it in the United States. What journalists report often provides the empirical evidence on which policymakers base their decisions, and their analyses are largely what inform the public's views. Despite their professional commitment to normative neutrality, journalists have personal opinions; indeed, their opinions shape their reporting, and thus help shape the opinions of others.

In a special edition of the center's bimonthly research bulletin, *Deadline,* that appeared in the summer of 1989, the center asked 23 leading American journalists, "Is the Cold War over or not, and—in either case—what are the consequences for journalism?" The question was posed to prominent columnists, reporters, and editors from both print and broadcast media. Their responses varied widely and in many cases were surprisingly candid, offering a unique look at the personal opinions of American journalists at a moment of fateful political transition. Offered on the eve of such momentous events as the breaching of the Berlin Wall and the Malta summit, their replies remain as revealing and important today as when they were offered, because it is precisely these events that these same journalists have been reporting through the perceptual filters they so candidly reveal in the remarks printed here. What they and their colleagues in the press continue to report in the future, moreover, will depend in no small part on the opinions of the 13 leading journalists whose contributions were selected for inclusion in this book.[1]

Surveying their answers, we were struck by the definitiveness with which many of these journalists—trained as they are to be objective observers who avoid expressing their own views—responded to a question that required an essentially subjective answer. "I don't think there is the slightest doubt that the Cold War . . . is definitively over," writes Hendrik Hertzberg, editor of the *New Republic,* one of the country's leading political magazines (which, despite a liberal editorial tradition, has become increasingly hostile to the Soviet Union in recent years). "Not only is the Cold War dead," writes Paul Quinn-Judge, former Moscow correspondent for the *Christian Science Monitor* and now with the *Boston Globe,* "but the Soviet system that we have known since World War II is being changed beyond recognition." Rod

Nordland, former deputy foreign editor of the Long Island, New York, daily *Newsday,* insists that the Cold War has ended "as surely as May follows April." Bill Monroe, editor of the *Washington Journalism Review,* goes even further: "'Cold War,' in fact, may be too limited a description of the historic scenery we are now leaving behind."

Equally striking is the precision with which some were ready to define the "end of the Cold War" in time and circumstance, this at a moment when the fall of the Berlin Wall had not yet occurred. Elizabeth Pond, former Moscow correspondent for the *Christian Science Monitor,* long considered one of the country's best dailies, writes that "the Cold War—the obsessive East-West confrontation—ended in the winter of 1988-1989 with Soviet withdrawal from Afghanistan and the announced withdrawal of 5,000 Soviet tanks from Eastern Europe." David Shipler, a Pulitzer Prize winner and former Moscow correspondent for *The New York Times,* writes that the Cold War "has been in the process of ending for about 15 years." He cites as both cause and symptom of this the SALT I treaty, the Apollo-Soyuz space mission, and U.S.-Soviet scientific cooperation. Michael Getler, assistant managing editor of the *Washington Post,* ties "the new era in international relations" directly to "the emergence of Mikhail Gorbachev." And James Chace, former managing editor of *Foreign Affairs,* attributes it to an "ideologically bankrupt and economically impoverished" Soviet Union that is now "suing for peace."

A few take exception: David Martin, Pentagon correspondent for CBS News—one of the major sources of news for many Americans—argues that "it is too soon to declare the Cold War over," with "thousands of nuclear missiles still pointed at one another, and with hundreds of thousands of troops still faced off against one another in central Europe." (He concedes, however, that "under Gorbachev there has been a profound change in U.S.-Soviet relations.") And, in a highly personal essay, Peter Gumbel, Moscow correspondent for the *Wall Street Journal,* complains that "just when people were saying it was over, the Cold War ambushed my wife the other day." After unwittingly straying into a zone closed to foreigners, he explains, she was nabbed by Moscow traffic police and interrogated for two hours. But among these two dozen reporters of diverse political and professional orientation a consensus does emerge: The Cold War is over. Most of the journalists, perhaps not surprisingly, agree with most of the policymakers.

But what does this mean for journalism and journalists? This is in some ways the much more interesting question. Do journalists believe that these changes—so obviously important for the making of national policy—have implications for the way they conduct their own business? The journalistic profession takes pride in its professionalism. It conducts itself according to a set of informal ethical and editorial standards, including a commitment to objectivity, fairness, and the representation of competing viewpoints. It takes very seriously its responsibility to report and explain events to the citizens who will then make choices about the conduct of the nation. In the context of such beliefs, we wanted to know if these journalists think that changes in the East-West relationship will require changes in the way international affairs are reported to the public.

On this question, a revealing split is evident. One group believes that the profession of journalism is already adequate to the new challenges of the post-Cold War era. Another holds that journalism, like American foreign policy, is facing a watershed and that new times require new ways of covering them.

Marvin Kalb, former Moscow correspondent for NBC News and currently director of the Joan Shorenstein Barone Center on the Press, Politics, and Public Policy at Harvard University, challenges what he terms the "widespread assumption that, with the change in U.S.-Soviet relations . . . there should in addition be a parallel change in the way American reporters cover the superpower relationship." Acknowledging that the new story of changing superpower relations is even richer than the old Cold War story and also deserving of greater coverage, Kalb nevertheless notes that "the reporter's job has not been changed." The job now, as before, he says, is not to be "a partisan for glasnost" or "a writer with a new set of political eyeshades," but simply "to dig, and keep digging." Bill Monroe, a former network newsman and now the editor of the *Washington Journalism Review,* answers in a similar vein. "How should Western journalists deal with these events?" he asks. "They should do, and they are doing, what comes naturally: Report them in all their breadth and depth and in all the fine, telling detail now so richly available. And in particular, they should give us chapter and verse on how those glorious . . . ideas of 1776 America are taking hold in the Soviet Union." Peter Braestrup, who covered Vietnam, Europe, and Africa for the *Washington Post* and the *New York Times* (and who is noted for his study criticizing the American press for helping lose the Vietnam War) criticizes the notion that reporting will change with the changing U.S.-Soviet relationship. For one thing, he writes, the "new" perspective is not all that new. "The Cold War prism has been crumbling for more than a decade," he notes. For another, "U.S. media coverage follows the flag. . . . For better or worse, the politicians will set the agenda, and the news media will follow." Braestrup also rejects the notion that the news media should listen to "those who demand steady attention to the global environment, human rights, and the Third World's plight. . . . The American news media—Cold War or no Cold War—cannot cover all problems, all countries, all plights."

For other journalists, however, the momentous changes under way in U.S.-Soviet relations, and their international repercussions, will require significant changes in the way American journalism covers the world. "What all this means for journalism," writes Hertzberg, of the *New Republic,* "is that news organizations are going to have to spend a lot more money. . . . The rest of the world suddenly becomes more important." Moreover, he argues, "The chief threat to human existence shifts from the Soviet-American nuclear standoff to the destruction of the environment." Robert Toth, national security correspondent for the *Los Angeles Times* and once its Moscow bureau chief, foresees a shift in focus, as well as in form: "The most important news will come less from Geneva and summitry than from Brussels and Pentagon-White House-Congress deliberations. These issues will be better suited to analytical pieces than to spot stories, demanding greater familiarity with details by reporters, and greater sympathy for complex but vital issues among editors." For Rod Nordland of *Newsweek,* journalists' "news priorities may now well change, and probably should, in Europe's favor. Europe is center stage again." (The central European revolts, half a year after he wrote those lines, lend additional force to his argument.)

For national security reporters, these changes may necessitate some intellectual retooling so that journalists can master subjects that have been obscured for years by the U.S.-Soviet focus of much news reporting. For Getler, who was one of the premier national security reporters before he became an editor, "the challenge will be to sense and report with precision on sweeping and complex changes around the world and to develop new expertise." As James Chace suggests, the growing interdependence of nations will require foreign correspondents "to familiarize themselves with the details of fiscal and monetary strategies as they once had to master the intricacies of arms control.

But for some, the ending of the Cold War implies more than merely practical changes. In an argument that comes close to self-criticsm, many such journalists maintain that the greater challenge for American journalism—which has so long been dominated by Cold War images, language, and frames of reference—will be to find a new analytical framework in which to report international events. As David Shaw, media reporter for the *Los Angeles Times,* writes, "For more than 40 years, American foreign policy has rested on this simple proposition: Anything the Soviet Union supported, the United States automatically opposed. Thus, like the Bush administration, American journalism must reevaluate both its priorities and strategies. It's time to begin covering the world on its own terms—not in Cold War, Soviet-missiles-on-the-horizon terms." For Shipler, "we are entering an era in which most of the postwar reflexes in international affairs will have to be cast away by journalists as well as diplomats." And as Thom Shanker, Pentagon correspondent for the *Chicago Tribune* (and its former Moscow bureau chief), writes, this new era presents "a unique opportunity for reporters to rewrite the rules of foreign and diplomatic correspondence. In a sense, the entire lexicon for reporting on Soviet politics is up for grabs."

What these journalists seem to be suggesting is that the "end of the Cold War" is more than a set of discrete events defined in time and place. Reading between the lines of their statements, we find them suggesting that what is really taking place is what the philosopher Thomas Kuhn has called a "paradigm shift." Such a shift occurs when an existing system of beliefs, values, and techniques employed to make sense of reality no longer suffices in the face of new evidence, forcing a revolutionary change in the way people understand their world.

In the realm of international relations, the end of the Cold War may be just as monumental a shift. New political, economic, and social facts are being created, and many of the journalists who are reporting them daily are finding their old theories about the world inadequate to explain what is now taking place within it. As the reporters of the new evidence that challenges the old paradigm, and as those who contribute every day to the lexicon that will ultimately articulate the new one, journalists bear a special responsibility, according to some. As David Shaw writes, "They must try to explain to an American public long conditioned to thinking of the Soviet Union as the enemy just how (and why) that country is changing (and not changing)." This is all the more difficult given that journalists, pressed for space and time, often must rely on familiar terminology to convey their meaning. Convenient as they are, all too often such terms are shorthand references that call up a whole host of assumptions that readers and viewers must now be encouraged to challenge. "When change is so fast," writes Flora Lewis of *The New York Times,* "the public has trouble absorbing it and tends to ask the wrong questions. . . . Balance has to mean more than intelligent, honest reporting. It also has to take account of the public's unspoken assumptions and address them where the news indicates that they should be corrected."

Developing an appropriate framework, lexicon, and—finally—paradigm, in the aftermath of the Cold War is a daunting challenge for journalism.[2] It requires the kind of self-scrutiny that many journalists expect the profession, with its cultivated skepticism, to resist. "The mainstream American press has never been very good at leading conceptually beyond the limitations of mainstream thinking in American society," writes David Shipler. "It would be healthier, especially in this time of immense fluidity, if journalists . . . opened their news columns to a greater array of unorthodox voices that could push back the horizons of imagination."

The consequences of a failure in this respect could be severe. "Screaming headlines" in the West about the momentous changes in the Soviet bloc, as Thomas Powers points out, could feed the fears of conservative opponents of glasnost and perestroika, compromising the chances for these policies' success. Better that reporters should seize glasnost, as David Martin suggests, as an "opportunity to report firsthand on . . . Soviet society" and thereby "challenge several generations' worth of preconceived notions."

"The world has for a long time been infinitely more complex than the old formulas," writes former White House spokeman Hodding Carter III, a journalist who fought for civil rights in the American South before coming to Washington as State Department spokesman. "Gorbachev's campaign for public criticism and institutional restructuring of his outmoded system is not a bad model for American journalism as well. Like the Soviet state, as presently constituted it is not up to the challenges posed by the world around it."

Peter Braestrup
(*Washington Post, The New York Times*)

The hope that an end to Soviet expansionism will lead to a "new age" of American news coverage of planet Earth seems to rest on two assumptions: (a) American journalists still view the world through a Cold War prism; and (b) American news executives, once freed from this confining East-West vision, will shift to a broader global agenda—environmental threats, human rights, hunger, and the plight of the Third World. Both assumptions seem a bit flawed.

First, the Cold War prism has been crumbling for more than a decade, since the breakup of the post-1945 foreign policy consensus during the Vietnam War. However, the earlier journalistic preoccupation with events growing out of the East-West contest was not irrational, while it lasted. The Soviets and their allies were directly involved in threatening activities in Europe, Asia, and elsewhere—and the West was responding. The "red menace," although imperfectly perceived and often exaggerated for domestic political purposes, was not simply a right-wing fantasy. The 1948-1949 Berlin blockade, the Berlin Wall, the Cuban missile crisis, Soviet support for Egypt and North Vietnam, the invasion of Afghanistan, the Korean War—these did occur. Stalin, Mao, Pol Pot, Ho Chi Minh, Castro, and Brezhnev were no Boy Scouts. Containment of communist expansionism was a story—an increasingly complicated story, but not an unnatural focus for American journalists.

But the fragmentation of the foreign policy consensus over Vietnam led to a different framework for journalists and politicians alike. Resisting Soviet ventures during the 1970s in Ethiopia, Angola, and Mozambique was a matter of debate in Congress; not all red menaces now seemed equally menacing. But in the early 1980s, when Central America became an East-West testing ground under the Reagan administration, both Congress and the press were divided over the region's significance. In short, after Vietnam, the major news organizations, by and large, showed little of the old alarm over all Marxist-Leninist inroads in the Third World.

This complaisance irked conservatives. For their part, those on the American left often criticized the media for their wariness toward the Soviet Union—and its Brezhnev-era arms buildup. The revelations since Gorbachev's rise to power indicate that the Soviets were, as Washington said, bent on achieving great-power status, gaining superiority in strategic weaponry, demoralizing NATO, and other unfriendly strategies. Thus, it would seem, the wariness was justified.

It may still be justified. But if the Cold War truly ends, one should not expect American news executives to set an agenda that will satisfy those who demand steady attention to the global environment, human rights, and the Third World's plight.

First, the American news media—Cold War or no Cold War—cannot cover all problems, all countries, and all plights. On average, American newspapers devote only 6 percent of their "news hole" to international news (versus 16 percent for sports). The high cost of overseas coverage has reduced the number of reporters deployed abroad by such giants as *Time, The New York Times,* and *Newsweek* since the mid-1960s. ABC, CBS and NBC, never strong overseas, are cutting back further.

It seems likely that in the future, as in the past, traditional journalistic practices will prevail. Novelty, conflict, and drama, real or impending, will not disappear as basic ingredients of news. Those regions of the earth where American interests or allies seem threatened by upheaval or disaffection (for example, Israel) will continue to get more attention than places that seem tranquil (Sweden) or simply irrelevant (Togo). And, it should be remembered that U.S. media coverage of the Third World does follow the flag. If the White House and Congress get worried about Zaire, so does the press. Only if the president takes the lead in words and action on a new foreign policy agenda will the U.S. media shift their attention to such matters. For better or worse, the politicians will set the agenda, and the news media will follow.

Hodding Carter III (former press secretary, the Carter administration)

American reporting, like American policy, has failed to reflect the fundamental shifts in economic, political, and even military reality that have occurred in the world over the past 15 years. Mesmerized by the long struggle with the Soviet Union, a struggle that has been the organizing principle and justification for most American actions abroad (and many at home) since World War II, we journalists have been slow to recognize that the postwar era is over. In trying to make his countrymen confront that fact, Gorbachev has done us the great favor of forcing us to do the same.

But if we are not careful, the disintegration of one outworn set of slogans could simply lead to the substitution of new, equally mindless ones—and of the kind of reporting that slogans, rather than careful scrutiny, produce.

It is true that there are today other major powers in the world that do not readily respond to the dictates of Moscow or Washington. It is true that the United States and the Soviet Union have severely damaged their economic prospects by pouring money and energy into military machinery that will never be used. And it is true that many of the important problems facing the United States, and the world generally, have nothing to do with the East-West equation. All of this has been true, moreover, at least since the mid-1970s.

But that does not mean that in the Gorbachev era—or in any era close at hand—the United States and the Soviet Union will cease to be relevant to each other or to other countries. Both remain great powers, with great-power interests and clients. Actions taken by one will continue to affect the other on a wide variety of fronts. In this new world, what is needed from American media is not less reporting from and about the Soviet Union, but more and better.

However, it is at least equally true that American journalists need to cover far more fully the smell and context of events throughout the world, from the Pacific Rim to the Common Market, from Latin America to Africa. The well-being of the United States is affected by decisions taken in an ever-expanding set of locales, but the American press corps that has been deployed to cover them has been shrinking steadily. Just as it has finally become inescapably obvious that Cold War cliches do not and cannot define reality, the megacorporations that control American journalism have decided that less is more when it comes to coverage everywhere.

Is the Cold War over? Sure, so much so that this has become the new conventional wisdom for right and left alike. And if we are not very careful, the new parrot-speak will produce as much mindlessness as the old. The world has for a long time been infinitely more complex than the old formulas. But you would have had a hard time understanding that if you relied on the typical news and commentary in the mass media. Gorbachev's campaign for public criticism and institutional restructuring of his outmoded system is not a bad model for American journalism as well. Like the Soviet state, as presently constituted it is not up to the challenges posed by the world around it.

Michael Getler (*Washington Post*)

The Cold War, as we have understood it for the past 40 years or so, is over, at least for now. It could return, of course, in some new but still recognizable form that feeds on latent mistrust in both the United States and the Soviet Union. The ending of regional wars in Afghanistan, the Persian Gulf, Southeast Asia, and southern Africa is attributable in part to exhaustion in addition to big-power pressures. So caution is called for.

But we are now, in my view, in the midst of an extraordinary moment in history, with unprecedented opportunities to produce a durable reduction in the superpower tensions and fears that have so dominated the postwar era.

The main reason for this new era in international relations, it seems to me, is the emergence of Mikhail Gorbachev. Ronald Reagan, whatever his flaws, also played an important role in bringing us to this point; in the end he sensed the uniqueness of Gorbachev and acted upon the opportunities. But it is precisely because of Gorbachev's uniqueness that looking ahead becomes so difficult. Much of what happens elsewhere in the world will depend on what happens in the Soviet Union.

It also will depend, though probably to a lesser degree, on whether the West, and the United States in particular, is imaginative in seizing the moment and shaping the relationship in a way that encourages the kind of Soviet reforms that will lead to a permanent end to the Cold War.

For journalists, the challenge will be to sense and report with precision on sweeping and complex changes around the world and to develop new expertise. The prospect of large cuts in strategic nuclear forces and the first withdrawals of American troops from Germany in 40 years will break patterns of thinking that so many of us have gotten used to. International security reporting will take on a new and broader face.

The collapse of Soviet communism as an economic or political model, the struggle for reform in the communist world, and the increased global focus on economic instead of military development and on market economies and pluralism rather than centrally planned economies are enormous stories. Are massive demonstrations in the non-Russian republics a sign that Gorbachev is in trouble, or that democratization is working? Do steps toward pluralism in Hungary and Poland mean that a new world is forming in Eastern Europe?

Economic and technological strength is in the ascendancy over purely military yardsticks in assessments of national security these days. "Star Wars" is giving way to trade wars. The economic challenge to the United States from Japan and elsewhere in Asia, and from a more integrated Europe after 1992, may well replace the military challenge from Moscow as the principal threat to America's sense of well-being.

For the first time, we may be seeing economic constraints in both the Soviet Union—with an economy that simply doesn't work—and the United States—with huge budget and trade deficits—working to encourage arms control. The arms control issues will also be expanding, from the traditional superpower missile balances to conventional forces, chemical weapons, and third-country combinations of missiles and chemical weapons.

Peter Gumbel (*Wall Street Journal*)

Just when people were saying it was over, the Cold War ambushed my wife the other day.

She drove into it. Visiting an artist friend who lives on the outskirts of Moscow, she unwittingly strayed into a zone closed to foreigners. She was nabbed by the next traffic cop, interrogated by unsavory types in leather jackets, denounced by "witnesses" she had never seen before, and then sent back with a stern warning.

For her, it was an unpleasant experience that dampened her enthusiasm for Moscow. For me, it was a sobering reminder that despite glasnost and perestroika, the Cold War still is far from over for journalists working here. Reporting from the Soviet Union undoubtedly has become easier. But most of the old Cold War barriers that were set up to isolate and control foreign correspondents are still in place. Until they are torn down, it will remain hard to cover the Soviet Union as anything other than an adversary.

Instead of being able to live alongside Russians, we are still forced to reside in foreigners' "ghettos." Militiamen stand at the entrances 24 hours a day, intimidating all but the bravest of our Soviet visitors. Our cars have special yellow number plates that prevent us from going anywhere unobtrusively. Most of the greater Moscow area beyond a ring road is closed to us.

Quite apart from generating personal feelings of being cooped up, these regulations greatly hinder our ability to report. Because we must give 48 hours' notice of our travel plans, the Soviet foreign ministry and local authorities can veto visits they deem inconvenient. For most of last year we were prevented from traveling to Armenia and Azerbaijan to report on the ethnic tension in those republics. This year, Moldavia has been off-limits for several weekends when big nationalist demonstrations were held, and Georgia was closed after troops clashed with protesters in April. (Similar Cold War rules apply to Soviet correspondents in the United States, who aren't supposed to stray beyond Washington, DC, and for whom several cities on the West Coast are permanently out of bounds.)

The Gorbachev era has undoubtedly ushered in some noticeable improvements for Moscow correspondents. It has become much easier to find Soviet sources. American journalists are rarely denounced anymore. Above all, the foreign ministry, given enough notice, has been letting us travel to some areas long closed. I was recently allowed to visit a town on the Chinese border, something that would have been unthinkable a few years ago.

Nonetheless, the Cold War will only be over for journalists when we can work in the Soviet Union as freely as in any other foreign posting. If the two superpowers are serious about improving relations, they should immediately agree to lift restrictions on our movements. We should be able to get on a plane or train or drive to any part of the country without having to give notice to anyone.

The CIA and the KGB may not be too thrilled about this, of course. To ease their fears, the process could perhaps be implemented gradually. Initially, all restrictions on travel in the greater Moscow area could be lifted, and we could be allowed to go—unannounced, and at any time—to the capitals of all 15 Soviet republics and big cities such as Leningrad. But ultimately, if the superpowers are serious about improving their relations and overcoming the suspicions of the past, they should override the objections of their spooks. After all, without some trust between the two sides, the Cold War will never end.

Hendrik Hertzberg (*New Republic*)

The United States and the Soviet Union still maintain huge military establishments with immense arsenals of nuclear and conventional weapons. They will continue to maintain them for many years to come—even if dramatic leaps in arms control are taken at the fastest conceivable speed. Even so, I don't think there is the slightest doubt that the Cold War, as that term has beeen understood for more than 40 years, is definitively over. The reason is the ideological death of totalitarianism.

The events that are unfolding in the Soviet Union are so vast in their implications that we in the West (and perhaps they in the East) have been unable to metabolize them. Perestroika may or may not "work," but glasnost, which is infinitely more important, has already "worked." Consider: the victories in contested, free elections of Andrei Sakharov, Roy Medvedev, Boris Yeltsin, and scores of other dissenters; the unconditional Soviet military withdrawal from Afghanistan; the publication of *1984, Darkness at Noon, Dr. Zhivago,* and multitudes of other once-forbidden books by Soviet and Russian authors living and dead, at home or in exile; the prospective publication of *The Gulag Archipelago* in *Novy Mir,* the Soviet Union's leading literary magazine; the crusading journalism of *Moscow News, Ogonyok, Argumenty i fakty,* and *Izvestia;* the surfacing of voluntary associations of every kind that, taken together, add up to a civil society; and, in Poland and Hungary, the immediate prospect of embryonic multiparty parliamentary democracy. The full list is much longer. What is important is that as recently as ten or even five years ago, not a single item on it would have been considered imaginable by the end of the twentieth century, if ever.

Revisionist quibbles aside, the basic cause of the Cold War was totalitarianism—more precisely, totalitarian ambition. The internal expression of totalitarian ambition was a determination to create, in countries already under communist rule, an all-powerful, all-seeing, perfectly wise state that would answer every human need and would therefore obviate and obliterate every competing human institution. The external expression of totalitarian ambition was a belief that all other social and political systems, judged by the standard of historical inevitability, were inferior and destined to die. This faith is now stone dead, and it cannot be brought back to life, ever. In the worst case, Gorbachev could fall; Soviet militarism could revive; civil liberties could be repressed; a form of Russian authoritarianism—a new czarism—could emerge. But the messianic, universalistic ideology that provided the underlying dynamic of an unending Cold War is as dead as the pharaohs.

What all this means for journalism is that news organizations are going to have to spend a lot more money. The immense changes that are taking place in the Soviet Union and Eastern Europe (and the consequent changes in Western Europe) are a better and richer story than the former stasis, even if the threat to American national security is considerably diminished. The rest of the world suddenly becomes more important—especially South America, which consists, as Ronald Reagan belatedly discovered, of "all different countries," none of them adequately covered by the Yankee press. Finally, the chief threat to human existence shifts from the Soviet-American nuclear standoff to the destruction of the environment. We can now pay serious attention to this, and not a moment too soon.

Marvin Kalb (former Moscow correspondent, NBC News)

There is a widespread assumption that, with the change in U.S.-Soviet relations spawned by glasnost, perestroika, and the zero-option missile treaty, there should in addition be a parallel change in the way American reporters cover the superpower relationship. Perhaps. On one level, to be sure, the change has already occurred. Reporting from the Soviet Union is richer, more multidimensional, more hopeful than at any other time since Lenin put his mark on Russian history more than 70 years ago. And reporting from

Washington reflects a new, more open approach to the Kremlin than at any time in recent decades. But, as one of my editors used to say, what else is new?

ABC News, quite appropriately, has added a second full-time correspondent to its Moscow bureau, and *The New York Times* and the *Washington Post* have dramatically expanded their coverage. During President Reagan's visit to Moscow in the spring of 1989, American anchormen prowled through the winding cobblestone streets of Moscow doing one interview after another with ordinary—and not so ordinary—Soviet citizens, who seemed to open their souls to these foreigners, sharing their once-secret aspirations and disappointments about their system and society. Suddenly, with satellites relaying live pictures back to the United States and the world, there was a succession of astonishing scenes: Gorbachev and Reagan strolling through a remarkably sunlit Red Square, sometimes with the American president's right arm draped over the Soviet leader's shoulder; Reagan lecturing hundreds of students at Moscow State University about the virtues of democracy and freedom; Dan Rather doing a quick street-corner interview with Gorbachev, no different, it seemed, from the days when he covered the White House; Peter Jennings, the Kremlin as his backdrop, chatting with a parade of Soviet officials; Tom Brokaw, doing his version of the new Russia, content in the knowledge that six months earlier he had done an hour's exclusive with the genie of glasnost. This was exceptional coverage—unprecedented, textured analyses of the new Soviet reality.

But in our collective wonder at the depth and breadth of the change, we should not lose sight of the fact that American reporters were doing what comes naturally to them. They were covering an extraordinary story.

During the height of the Cold War, earlier generations covered extraordinary stories, too—important summits in 1955, 1961, and 1967; the Cuban missile crisis; and occasional flare-ups of high tension and nuclear alerts in the 1970s. It is true that many reporters focused on these moments of tension. The Cold War in its many faces was, after all, the story. There were other reporters who tried to focus on Soviet politics, economics, and literature. Soviet officials didn't make it easy, and home interest was minimal. There was censorship in Moscow until April 1961, and then there was self-censorship, allowing little latitude for creative, enterprising journalism. The windows were shut on the world, opened only on occasion for a specific state purpose, and then shut again. Sometimes there was a fluke, such as Khrushchev's diaries, obtained and published by *Time,* a sensational scoop. But in that Russia, as contrasted wtih Gorbachev's, such a scoop was a rare and wonderful thing. Then—as now—the reporter's job was to dig, and keep digging, accumulating nuggets of insight and information about the Soviet Union, the superpower tangle, and the fascination of successive U.S. presidents with the alternating threats, teases, and promises of Stalin and his succcessors.

Gorbachev has launched a revolution, no doubt. It is a gripping news story, but it's also very complicated. One Soviet friend, a cynic, says that the Soviet Union is the only country in the world where democracy is imposed from above. The view that the USSR was a static society before Gorbachev, and that now something wholly new is being created, is misleading. The Soviet Union has been changing; the logical question now is whether it has changed.

What is clear is that the reporter's job has not been changed by Gorbachev, nor by the massive changes in our perception of the superpower relationship, from a wary uneasiness—a keep-up-your-dukes approach to the Soviets—to a warm embrace of the comforting notion that the Cold War is over. If, in this new era, the reporter gets greater access to the story, he or she should take full professional advantage of the opportunity. Editors and producers should provide the time and space for the exceptional coverage that is now possible. New vistas are open, new stories, too—environment, health care, the conquest of space.

The times require special effort not just from American reporters, but from their Soviet sources as well. Traditional horizons of thought and attitude are being pushed back so rapidly that, for example, Soviet novelists and poets do not have a chance to write; they are too busy being journalists. "Every night, on television, in the papers, there's something new," Yevgeny Yevtushenko recently told Craig Whitney of *The New York Times.* "People want us to help them, to speak for them—they have to call on poets to do it, because we have no politicians in our country. And if we stop fighting to go off and write a novel, maybe you'll find the freedom has been cut off."

Sergei Baruzdin, editor of the Soviet literary journal *Druzhba Naradov,* explained: "The journalistic forms—articles, essays, expository prose—may be as good as the classic short story or tale used to be. Maybe we need journalism more just now." Pushkin, Tolstoy, Gogol, and Dostoevsky all turned away from literary form to public activity in their day, too.

This is a glorious moment for the American reporter who knows Russian, loves pumpernickel bread, and has read Dostoevsky.

American reporters are not novelists, but Russian novelists can be great sources of information for them. There can be no mistaking roles, however. The American reporter is not a partisan for glasnost, nor a writer with a new set of political eyeshades. The reporter is again covering a story—but what a story!

Flora Lewis (*The New York Times*)

The Cold War didn't start one morning with an artillery barrage and tanks chugging across borders. And it won't end with an armistice and a surrender document. That's why we've called it the Cold War—a state of armed confrontation without actual shooting. Both U.S. and Soviet forces have engaged in foreign combat since it began, but not against each other. However, military planning in both East and West has focused primarily on this confrontation for two generations. And a lot of the other activities associated with wartime have been undertaken more or less energetically throughout the period—espionage, propaganda, economic mobilization and denial, political maneuvering.

All that won't just stop on a day somebody announces peace. We don't even have a standard to measure or identify such a day. We are in a period of historic transformation, but it is incremental, full of uncertainties and contradictions, changing rapidly in some ways and scarcely at all in others. Of course, that is much harder to report and analyze than something you can represent with pins on a map. Subtleties matter immensely. There is a vast ripple effect beyond the direct impact of changing Soviet-American, or even East-West, relations. It affects such things as the view of Salvadorean rebels on the objectives and possible achievements of armed insurrection, the attitudes of the far left and the far right in West Germany about their country's appropriate role in the world and its definition as a nation, the development plans of Angolan revolutionaries who once thought winning was enough. The very idea of social engineering is being reopened to question.

All this is hard news, but it doesn't have an easily defined cutting edge. Things overlap and have to be added up in a series of shifting contexts where their interrelations aren't clear. Do we paint too broad a picture, losing sight of all important details that refute the general impression? Do we take too narrow an approach, magnifying personalities to the neglect of political climate, economic pressures, and historical influences, which make a significant difference?

When change is so fast, the public has trouble absorbing it and tends to ask the wrong questions. Will Gorbachev win out over his opposition? Can the Soviets really change? Are they getting democracy and won't that make them just like us? Journalism needs to recognize what is wrong with the questions, and explain that, so that the answers it reports can be understood. A lot of people underestimate the profound importance of what is going on in the communist world and insist on the past as a guide. Others overestimate the process of change and what it can accomplish. Balance has to mean more than intelligent, honest reporting. It also has to mean taking account of the public's unspoken assumptions and addressing them where the news indicates that they should be corrected.

Perhaps the most difficult problem for journalism can be summarized as the presentation of interdependence, not only of different parts of the world, but of different topics and issues; for example, the relation of military security and economic concerns, of environmental problems and sociocultural attitudes. How do you break all this into compartments that can be handled effectively, specifically enough to convey real information and not just vague simplicities, and at the same time include all the crucial links?

As a foreign correspondent, I've long felt that finding the question is the key. The answers you get depend on that. You have to keep reshaping it, refining it, adjusting it to events and attitudes. That has to be done more than ever in this fascinating period.

Postscript (December 30, 1989)

As the dramatic events of 1989 developed, it also became clear that the role of journalists from the communist countries was changing profoundly and had a great significance in the ending of the Cold War. This became evident not only within each of their countries—the local press is always an important source for foreign correspondents—but also for international reporting.

The most impressive example came with the uprising in Romania. Because of the regime's hostility to the Western press and its tight controls, there were hardly any Western correspondents on the spot or able to arrrive quickly when the news broke. We had more or less forgotten that of course Soviet-bloc journalists were regularly stationed there. But suddenly they became a major source of information, reporting straightforwardly, directly and, so far as we could tell, as accurately as any professional reporters. The Romanian television and news agency performed notably, but so did others, including TASS and the Hungarian, Yugoslav, and other correspondents, and the rest of the world relied on them for several crucial days.

I can think of no more telling example of post-Cold War cooperation than this case of common appreciation of objective reporting.

David Martin (*Wall Street Journal*)

Thousands of nuclear missiles and hundreds of thousands of troops are still amassed on each side, yet the Cold War seems for all intents and purposes to be over, thanks to the stunning political transformation of Eastern Europe, which has effectively neutered the Warsaw Pact. On paper, the forces of the Warsaw Pact are only marginally less threatening than they were a year ago, but in fact not even the worst-case scenario foresees the new governments of Eastern Europe mounting a military threat against the West. The arms control proposals now on the table—a 50 percent cut in strategic weapons, a 275,000-man ceiling on U.S. and Soviet troops in Europe—seem paltry compared to the political events they are supposed to reflect. It's impossible to predict the future course of East-West relations, but it is safe to say that the notion of military confrontation seems increasingly farfetched. A world in which a U.S. secretary of state says the United States would not object if Soviet troops were to help restore order in Romania is a fundamentally different world.

That does not change the fundamental assumption under which most of us who cover national security operate—namely, that the relationship between the United States and the Soviet Union is the number one news story. If anything, it makes the story bigger because change is what news is all about. Major developments in U.S.-Soviet relations are likely to take the form of negotiations, not confrontations, but it does not follow that the story will become the exclusive property of diplomatic correspondents and that Pentagon reporters like myself had better look elsewhere for news. Those negotiations seem likely to produce such deep cuts in the levels of armaments that the United States and its allies will be forced to rethink their entire defense strategy. What happens, for instance, when the United States starts pulling troops out of Europe? Should the United States continue to invest billions of dollars in the effort to make its land-based missiles invulnerable against the increasingly improbable scenario of a Soviet first strike? From a reporter's standpoint, these stories are much more interesting than the standard U.S.-Soviet story of ships going bump in the night. The problem will be finding the time to tell them on the air.

As for our coverage of the Third World, that will probably suffer. Most of the stories we do about the Third World are done in the context of proxy superpower confrontations—Afghanistan, Angola, Cambodia, Nicaragua. Without those confrontations, I think reporting interest will quickly dwindle (except where—in Panama, for instance—American lives are at stake). However, this will be offset by more reporting on the Soviet Union, as Western journalists continue to gain access to what used to be off-limits. Pentagon reporters in particular should take advantage of glasnost to bombard the Soviet embassy with requests to visit Soviet military units and, more importantly, to talk to Soviet military leaders. The opportunity to report firsthand on the Soviet military and the rest of Soviet society is an opportunity to challenge several generations' worth of preconceived notions.

Bill Monroe (*Washington Journalism Review*)

As long as the United States and the Soviet Union remain the preeminent scorpions of our little planet, somebody will want to define the phrase *Cold War* as applying to that irreducible level of tension that must exist between them. Defined in that way, the Cold War is not over. Certainly the United States will not be able to stake its security anytime soon on simple trust.

But something has ended—or is ending. Let the historians put a name to it. "Cold War," in fact, may be too limited a description of the historic scenery we are now leaving behind.

There are those who say nothing has ended because, if Gorbachev fails, the Soviets will revert to truncheon and missile. Probably so. But this is a small, short-range truth irrelevant to the greater truth behind it: Gorbachev is not a rootless, aberrational phenomenon. He is the Soviet advocate for a global tide of history favoring political and economic freedoms, a tide that has been gaining strength inside the Soviet Union at least since the time of Khrushchev.

More important than Gorbachev by far, and more reliable, are those ideas about free speech, representative government, and free markets that have been making converts in the Soviet Union. When Gorbachev departs, whenever and however, those ideas will remain rooted in Soviet soil—the very same troublesome ideas that excite the students of China and Lech Walesa's durable militants in Poland. If Gorbachev fails, the ideas he speaks for will march on to a future rendezvous with a new Gorbachev in the twenty-first century.

The Soviets held at gunpoint since World War II a few small, sullen satellites. The West, on the other hand, by the uses of freedom, has converted the two military juggernauts responsible for World War II, Germany and Japan, into great, stable, productive nations allied with the West. And the fuel of capitalist incentives has lit up other conspicuous gems of prosperity: Korea, Singapore, Taiwan, Hong Kong.

None of this has been lost on the stagnant world of communism. Khrushchev, denouncing Stalinism and economic rigidity, was a prophet of glasnost and perestroika 30 years ago. Deng Xiaoping openly departed from Marxism when he began leasing land to peasants. And all of those thousands upon thousands of free-world intellectuals who were certain 40 years ago that communism owned the future are now dead or quiet.

One phase of the half-century now ending is the ideological contest between communism and democracy. Democracy has won it.

Another aspect of the waning epoch is the pragmatic economic rivalry between centralized and free-market systems. Deng Xiaoping and Gorbachev have testified that the West has won it.

And a third basic component of recent history that is probably ending (this will be clearer in a decade or two) is Soviet expansionism, recoiling from the shock of Afghanistan and the crunch of domestic economic crisis.

How should Western journalists deal with these events? They should do, and they are doing, what comes naturally: Report them in all their breadth and depth and in all the fine, telling detail now so richly available. And in particular, they should give us chapter and verse on how those gloriously ancient, wonderfully new ideas of 1776 America are taking hold in the Soviet Union with a potential for subverting authoritarianism that no American defense budget could ever match. These passionate, explosive notions—not miraculous weaponry—hold the real promise of peace for our grandchildren.

Only fifty years ago, the cancerous nationalism and technological genius of Germany and Japan plunged the world into horrific warfare. Our problems today with those former enemies focus on economic competition and trade, infinitely more manageable problems than the threat of nuclear war. Considering what we have seen happen to Germany and Japan in our lifetime, and considering what is happening now in Moscow, Western reporters should examine the prospect that eventually, our security does not depend on the hope of Soviet failure. It depends on the hope of Soviet success. Gorbachev is on our side preceisely because he is on the side of the Soviet people.

Paul Quinn-Judge (*Boston Globe*)

Western journalists, like many Western political leaders, are still tempted to hide behind intellectual complacency when they look at the Soviet Union. (I would argue that Western—particularly American—political leaders suffer from this much more than journalists, but that's another story.) We say Gorbachev's reforms are not working, he is under pressure from party conservatives, communism as an ideology is dead.

All this may well be true. We can certainly find plenty of Soviet intellectuals who will tell us the same thing. But we tend to avoid the fundamental issue: Not only is the Cold War dead, but the Soviet system that we have known since World War II is being changed beyond recognition. The regular announcements in the West that Soviet reform is faltering and that Gorbachev will be gone in two more years are, quite frankly, a cop-out. We should neither support nor decry perestroika. We should seize the opportunity that foreign journalists here have not had for sixty years: the chance to go beyond the "what" and "when" of news gathering and look at the processes that are shaping change. Until a few years ago, change in the Soviet Union was glacial. Now we see a country where the most fundamental and cherished assumptions—in politics, economics, history, and literature—can and do change completely in a matter of months. It's worth remembering that in February 1986 Gorbachev told French journalists that Stalinism was a concept invented by opponents of communism to blacken the Soviet Union. And last November ideology chief Vadim Medvedev declared its total opposition to the writings of Solzhenitsyn. Now it appears *The Gulag Archipelago* may be out here in time for Medvedev's summer vacation.

The weakness of perestroika is that it is reform by an elite, in this case a remarkably small one. When this elite tries to push proposals through the bureaucracy, it encounters massive problems. But its very smallness makes it easier for it to generate unorthodox ideas. Some of these, such as the call for the total abolition of nuclear weapons, are routinely dismissed in the West as propaganda. But perhaps they are not propaganda—they may just be the expression of the genuine beliefs of the present reforming elite. Perhaps we should start looking at them seriously and asking what the practical implications of such proposals would be.

One of the underlying assumptions of Gorbachev's reforms appears to be a willingness to sacrifice some military might in the hope of revitalizing ideology and the economy. (The Soviets may even, eventually, be willing to shed much of their control over Eastern Europe.) The chances of such dramatic reforms actually succeeding are quite low, but we should already be trying to gauge the impact of a revitalized, dynamic Soviet Union on the rest of the world.

If reform fails, the consequences for ordinary Soviets, and perhaps the rest of us, will be grim. In any case, we will need to understand the processes that will have either molded change or led to the rejection of Gorbachev's policies.

Harrison Salisbury (*The New York Times*)

During the Cold War, which was raging at its very peak when I went to Moscow for *The New York Times,* it was literally impossible for me to report anything that was not the subject of controversy. Every dispatch I wrote had to clear the censors in Moscow, and very often they did not. Those that got through often became the subject of controversy in New York, attracting letters from readers who felt that the very presence of a reporter in Moscow was per se evidence of partisanship.

These things would strike today's audience as baroque. We don't think of the tensions and the divisions between the two countries in terms nearly so severe as those of forty years ago. Nonetheless, there are plenty of tensions that do remain and plenty of difficulties for the correspondent attempting to give readers some coherence and knowledge of how things do change. One must recognize that there was a considerable period of time in which Gorbachev was initiating one change after another, one new attitude after another, and although these were reported, they were reported with skepticism and were received in the American public with equal skepticism because of an unwillingness to believe that change actually had occurred. This is not unusual. When Stalin died, almost immediately his heirs attempted to distance themselves from the most extreme facets of his policy. When I began to report these various changes, the *Times* played down the stories and sometimes didn't carry them at all because they were afraid they would give the wrong impression—that things were changing in the Soviet Union. But things do change in the Soviet Union, just as they change here. As we see now, the Soviet Union is susceptible to extraordinary changes, which is a very positive fact, one we might be expected to greet with great joy. Increasingly in this country, I think we are beginning to open up and say that "something is happening there"—although the next questions are usually "How long will it last?" and "Will it change back again?" Those are perfectly legitimate questions, because changes don't always go in just one way, and the question of whether Gorbachev can survive the diet of severe changes he is imposing on the USSR is a valid and reasonable one. But we have now reached the point at which we see free, or practically free, elections—which are much more free than in some of our own client states, and which in terms of the Soviet Union are radical and revolutionary. And we see all kinds of stirrings and demands for greater freedom and autonomy, which imply further change. Will it happen or will it not? We don't know. That's the next episode, one we must watch very closely.

We owe a great debt now to the correspondents in Moscow, because they have established in our minds the changes going on. This is particularly important for such big issues as disarmament and the arms race and the relationship between the United States and the Soviet Union, because progress that will be made in those areas is almost entirely conditioned by the overall climate of opinion, both in the Soviet Union and in the United States.

Having spent some forty years in this field, I think that the most important thing for progress is the basic atmospherics of both countries. It isn't enough just to change. People must feel the change and then begin to reciprocate—to say that under these conditions it is possible for us to go ahead and propose this and that and negotiate this and that—and perhaps to create a better and more secure, safer and saner world.

David Shaw (*Los Angeles Times*)

George Kennan says the time for regarding the Soviet Union "primarily as a possible, if not probable, military opponent . . . has clearly passed," and there is no question that evidence of fundamental change in the Soviet Union is as abundant as it is incontrovertible: glasnost, perestroika, economic decentralizing, greater freedom of speech, the first contested national elections since the revolution of 1917, political settlements in Cambodia and Angola, the withdrawal of Soviet troops from Afghanistan, and reductions in Soviet military forces in central Europe. Is the Cold War over? *The New York Times* says so on its editorial page and, on its front page, publishes a story with the stunning (but accurate) observation that after three days of talks in Cuba, Mikhail Gorbachev was leaving Havana and Fidel Castro for London and "the more congenial company of Prime Minister Margaret Thatcher."

What does all this mean for American journalists? John Kohan, Moscow bureau chief for *Time,* says, "There are opportunities for journalists that would have been unthinkable a few years ago." He's right, of course. American journalists in the Soviet Union may now explore and travel and question in a way never before possible. That's the opportunity. The challenge is a bit more complicated.

Journalists reporting from inside the Soviet Union must first capitalize on their unprecedented access. They must try to explain to an American public long conditioned to thinking of the Soviet Union as the enemy just how (and why) that country is changing (and not changing), and what all this portends, in individual and global terms. But they must also—like journalists everywhere—retain their congenital skepticism about all promises and seemingly beneficial change, even as their gratitude for an excitement over these changes mounts.

Editors in the United States have a still greater challenge. Somehow, in an era of tightened news budgets and America's self-absorption with its own diminished economic power, they must seize this occasion to broaden their foreign coverage. For too long, foreign coverage in the American press has been insular and jingoistically solipsistic—concerned almost exclusively with how events abroad affect life here. Because nothing could possibly affect life here more than nuclear war, that threat has been the implicit focus of too much foreign coverage, whether from the perceived source of that threat (the Soviet Union itself) or from Vietnam, the Middle East, or Latin

America. For more than forty years, American foreign policy has rested on this simple proposition: Anything the Soviet Union supported, the United States automatically opposed. Thus, like the Bush administration, American journalism must reevaluate both its priorities and its strategies. It's time to begin covering the world on its own terms—not in Cold War, Soviet-missiles-on-the-horizon terms—and to give American readers a comprehensive and visceral sense of what life is like for people who live in other countries. This is especially true of coverage in those Third World countries so long ignored by most of the American press. But it is also true of other areas of the world where the potential for a superpower clash has long been a dominant theme, whether militarily (as in Europe and the Middle East) or ideologically (as in Latin America).

This opportunity for reevaluation could not come at a more important moment. With the impending commercial unification of Europe, the modified stance of the PLO, and the growing power of Japan, there is a great deal to be covered abroad. Let's hope that the American press—like the American public, so long indifferent to most of what happens beyond our shores—is up to the challenge.

David K. Shipler (*The New York Times*)

If "Cold War" means a nonshooting relationship of absolute hostility between the superpowers, then it has been in the process of ending for about 15 years. In the 1970s the SALT I treaty, the Apollo-Soyuz space mission, and the efforts at scientific cooperation were among the landmarks along a bumpy and circuitous road toward a discovery of the common ground that the United States and the Soviet Union share. The regression provoked by the invasion of Afghanistan and the archconservatism of the first Reagan administration turned out to be a temporary detour from that basic path, and the advance has now been accelerated dramatically by the liberalization in Soviet domestic and foreign policy brought by Mikhail Gorbachev.

The implications are enormous for American journalism's coverage of East-West issues, internal Soviet developments, and interactions between the Third World and industrialized nations. If Gorbachev's United Nations address last December represented his true vision of the world's emerging power relationships, and if Washington responds imaginatively, then we are entering an era in which most of the postwar reflexes in international affairs will have to be cast away—by journalists as well as diplomats.

No longer will U.S.-Soviet competition in the Third World be a zero-sum game in which every Soviet gain means an American loss, and vice versa. In the Persian Gulf, Afghanistan, Angola, Cambodia, the Middle East, and perhaps even Central America, there have been and will be overlapping interests, parallel objectives, and increasing space for U.S.-Soviet cooperation. These prospects should be as newsworthy as the confrontations have been.

The mainstream American press has never been very good at leading conceptually beyond the limitations of mainstream thinking in American society. Reporters writing about foreign affairs cover government primarily; mostly they quote officials, or a few anointed scholars and think-tank analysts who rarely break out of the parameters of consensus. This is natural, even logical, but it has a sterilizing effect on public debate. It would be healthier, especially in this time of immense fluidity, if journalists wrote more skeptically and creatively about the big issues and opened their news columns to a greater array of unorthodox voices that could push back the horizons of imagination.

One danger is the propensity of the press to personify policy; to portray Gorbachev, for example, not merely as the catalyst of liberalization but as its sole source and practitioner. This is dramatic, but it masks the extensive societal roots of the change and the weight of continuity. It may also lead to swings between euphoria and despair—euphoria as Gorbachev gains power, despair if he falls. It fails to recognize the longer rhythms of history that are in play here, the importance of what does not change, of what is not new.

Notes

1. The complete collection of essays, many of which are cited in this introduction, is found in "The 'End' of the Cold War? The Coming Challenge for Journalism," *Deadline,* Summer, 1989.

2. In an attempt to come to terms with both the structural challenges and unprecedented opportunities that accompany glasnost and perestroika, the 25 American media organizations with Moscow bureaus have increased the number of their Moscow correspondents by some 25 percent, to 49 from 40, between 1989 and 1990. Seven of the bureaus have expanded their reporting staffs, and one, *The Boston Globe,* has opened its first Moscow bureau. The American Moscow press corps is also a better trained group than in the past, with all but six of its members having received some Russian language training prior to arrival and almost half having undertaken some advanced study of the Soviet Union or international relations. In September 1989, the first professional Sovietologist was named to the Moscow press corps when CBS News posted Jonathan Sanders, previously the assistant director of Columbia University's Harriman Institute for the Advanced Study of the Soviet Union, to the Moscow beat. Further information on the U.S. press corps in Moscow, and detailed biographical notes on each of its members, will be found in the "1990 Moscow Press Corps Who's Who," in *Deadline,* March/April, 1990, pp. 5-12.

15

The End of the Cold War: Views from Leading Soviet International Commentators

YASSEN N. ZASSOURSKY

All 13 Soviet contributors to this chapter belong to the elite of Soviet international journalism. They represent major daily newspapers, weekly magazines, news agencies, and broadcasting. All of them agree that dramatic changes in international relations have abolished Soviet-American confrontation and dramatically transformed communication channels throughout the world. However, they differ quite emphatically in their verdict as to the end of the Cold War—from Alexander Pumpyansky, the deputy editor of the *Novoye Vremya* (*New Times*) newsmagazine, for whom the Cold War is over, to Yuri Zhukov, the veteran *Pravda* international commentator, for whom the Cold War started in October 1917 and for whom it remains.

The variety of attitudes reflects the diversity of approaches, though some generalizations can be made. First, those who were especially active in the Cold War rhetoric are less categoric in asserting the end of the Cold War. Second, most of the interviewed Soviet journalists try to identify ways of improving professional standards. Third, a lot of attention is being focused on the areas and problems that might promote confrontational attitudes.

Alexander Bovin, the well-known and vocal *Izvestia* columnist, is concerned with the problems of the Third World. Gennadi Gerasimov, the Soviet Foreign Ministry spokesman who worked for several years as the New York correspondent for the APN news agency and whose ironic and caustic remarks made him famous far beyond the Soviet borders, insists that there are no winners in the Cold War.

Stanislav Kondrashov, who was the *Izvestia* correspondent in Washington and has published several books on the United States, tries to dig into the philosophical aspects of the Cold War mentality. And Vitaly Korotich, the charismatic editor-in-chief of the popular *Ogonyok* magazine, asserts that the Cold War has always existed and will continue in the future because of the vested interests of the military establishment. Valentin Zorin, the popular television commentator who interviewed both President George Bush and President Mikhail S. Gorbachev, regretfully believes that journalism will be the last fortification of the Cold War.

Alexander Pumpyansky, the deputy editor-in-chief of the *Novoye Vremya* newsmagazine who spent some time in the United States as the *Komsomolskaya Pravda* newspaper correspondent, predicts that the Cold War will be followed by the Cold Peace. Yuri Romantsov, the deputy general director of TASS who headed the TASS bureau in New York City, is concerned with the professional aspects of international journalism and communciation. Nikolai Setunski, editor-in-chief of the *Eho Planety* newsmagazine and former TASS correspondent in the United States, warns that the end of the Cold War might not be irreversible.

Yuri Zhukov views the Cold War as an inescapable component of the present international relations that could only get either aggravated or relaxed, as is the case now. Leonid Zolotarevsky, a leading Soviet television journalist who served as the Soviet anchor in the Supreme Soviet-American Congress television spacebridges, agrees with Yuri Zhukov that the Cold War started in October 1917, and looks at ways to overcome the mentality of the Cold War. Vsevolod Ovchinnikov, the international *Pravda* commentator who served as correspondent in Japan and Great Britain, views martial military power as a potential source of the Cold War.

Finally, Professor Spartak Beglov, a leading political analyst for the APN news agency who is at this time the APN correspondent in London, discusses historical and theoretical aspects of the international communication policies and pleads for a new and fresh start in international coverage in the media.

The Soviet journalists are quite cautious in their approaches to the dynamics of international relations, but they leave no doubts about their negative views of the mentality, stereotypes, and attitudes of the Cold War. They also are very vocal about their own faults in the best tradition of glasnost, proving once again that the changes in the Soviet media and journalism seem to be irreversible for the benefit of international understanding and mutual trust.

Spartak Beglov (APN News Agency)

The Cold War started right after the October Revolution, becoming especially evident in the sphere of propaganda. Comintern used to be the headquarters of such activities. The U.S. and Soviet governments were not at first parts of it; at least, this was true regarding *our* administration. The reason was, I think, the existence of close bilateral economic cooperation.

The essence of the Cold War is in each side's creation of an enemy image of the other side. The Cold War is a view of the historical imcompatibility of the two systems, when each confrontation is represented as good versus evil. The Cold War stopped during World War II and resumed after 1945 due to the ideological incompatibility.

Every stage of the Cold War had its stereotypes. Before World War II, the West promoted the Bolshevik as the enemy of liberty; we pictured the West as the land of the "yellow devil." After the war, one side was talking about the "iron curtain" and Soviet expansion, the other about espionage and aggressiveness. The Cold War twisted other forms of communication as well, including cultural ties and people exchanges.

The 20th CPSU Congress in 1956 delivered the first blow of the Cold War. The congress said the "hot war" was not inevitable and it destroyed Stalin's legacy of the enemy image as the initiator of nuclear war. But the situation remained paradoxical in the USSR; some forces were generating the enemy image while others were destroying it.

This went on until 1986, until Geneva, with President Reagan participating as an advocate of the Cold War. The political climax of the Cold War was Reagan's declaration of the Soviet Union as the "evil empire" in 1983. The beginning of its end was his declaration that he changed his mind.

At the very beginning of this end were "Gorbachev seminars," that is, his informal talks with Western leaders, the first of which was his meeting with Mrs. Thatcher in London in December 1984. When Gorbachev actually described his "new thinking" concept. Thatcher tapped him on the shoulder and said, "We can do business with him." That was the beginning. The end of the transitional period from the Cold War to the "new thinking" was marked by President Bush saying he staked on perestroika, on Gorbachev.

The major task of Soviet mass media now is propaganda—not of the world revolution or of peaceful coexistence as a form of class struggle—but that of the "new thinking," its developments and concrete definition. The "new thinking" is in the interests of the whole world.

With the start of glasnost it became much easier for Soviet journalists to do their jobs. The leaders of the Foreign Ministry became accessible. A new stage in international journalism might begin when the forming of Soviet foreign policy becomes the business of the parliament. With new parties forming, different views on foreign policy will become a common occurrence, a stage of real pluralism.

Actually, there remain no serious restrictions for foreign correspondents in the USSR. One of the only hindrances left is of a different character: Those journalists who support Mr. Gorbachev do not dare criticize the politics of the initiator of glasnost and perestroika.

Alexander Bovin (*Izvestia*)

I think that within one year the Cold War will be over. The fall of the Berlin Wall is the symbol of this. In fact, Soviet-American rapprochement and real prospects for a substantial cutback in conventional and nuclear weapons signal the beginning of the end of the Cold War.

Another good omen is the development by the two opposing systems of a method to stop regional conflicts. It was realized in Namibia and can be useful in Angola, Mozambique, and Afghanistan. We are witnesses to new approaches in reaching "national compromises." The term *national* is not a good one; instead it should be "social" or "class" compromises. The third sign of the end of the Cold War is purely European. We see the end of a Yalta-ordered Europe and the birth of a different Europe that is not yet clear-cut. The last pages of postwar history are being written.

These three signals marking the end of the Cold War represent good news for Europe and the whole world. What remains is the force of inertia. For the United States, Central America is a backyard, a fact proven by the recent actions in Panama. The USSR may, of course, make a surprise move of some kind. But that would be a zigzag—a step back from the current direction. The dominant tendency is the gradual end of confrontation.

Any possible future conflicts connected with the German situation, Transylvania, or Polish border demarcations will not contain the main element of the Cold War: face-to-face confrontations between the two systems. Any conflicts from now on will be "independent" ones that will not have the United States or the USSR behind them. The Third World is no longer considered merely a sphere to be divided between the first two worlds. Under these circumstances, it will be easier to extinguish or even prevent regional conflicts.

I believe that once we have resolved the domestic problems within my country we shall play a more active role in the world arena. Our weakness is obvious to the whole world. The Americans do not want to offend us, although the invasion of Panama may have been a U.S. reaction to our weakness. We were having problems in the Baltic republics and in Transcaucasia and could not react to the Panama events. Now only America is a superpower. But America will be more subdued when we rise to our feet.

Regarding our "shop matters," the Cold War has not removed all obstacles in the reporter's work. It is still hard to publish articles about North Korea, Mozambique (and the hell that goes on in that country), or Syria. But the removal of these obstacles is an ongoing process, as is the end of the Cold War.

Gennadi Gerasimov (Soviet government spokesman)

When we define the term *Cold War,* we understand it to be a state of confrontation between East and West. Before the Malta summit, I predicted the burial of the Cold War there. When in Malta, Mikhail Gorbachev said that we did not see the United States as an enemy and would never start a war against it. President Bush declared in January 1990 that the United States would not attack the Soviet Union. That is why from this point on we can speak about the end of the Cold War.

On the other hand, we are still laden with old impressions. A recent poll published by the *Christian Science Monitor* showed that only 18 percent of Americans confirm the Cold War's end. The remaining 80 percent do not rush to this conclusion and think that the changes in the Soviet Union may be reversed. The skeptics believe that unless we improve our economic situation, a return to the old practice is possible. The idea of communism as an absolute evil is ingrained so deeply in the heart of many Americans that they are waiting for additional assurances.

In light of the drastic changes in Eastern Europe, the Cold War fortifications have fallen. Everybody in Western Europe also agrees that the menace from the East has disappeared. Then why maintain the present arms level? The arms control talks are evidently behind schedule.

Stability in Europe should no longer be based upon nuclear deterrence but rather upon a common-home concept. To say that radical changes in the East are responsible for destabilizing the general situation is to be a hostage of Cold War thinking. We must think in the categories of the European confederation creation's epoch. Such an approach would be a continuation of the process begun with the Helsinki accords. With this in mind, a "Helsinki-2" summit was proposed to be held in 1990. In this context I see no winners in the Cold War. It is simply over.

In Moscow there are currently 580 foreign reporters, all fine professionals whose successful work here is usually an important step in their careers.

While we have removed many of the restrictions on foreign journalists, some of the restrictions—those similar to ones imposed upon Soviet correspondents in, say, the United States, Great Britain, and France—remain. But I expect they will be removed in due time.

One of the remaining barriers for foreign journalists in the USSR is the existence of restricted areas. Some of the districts are closed, not for security reasons but, I believe, because of bad roads, poor-quality hotels, and the like. We should not have to be ashamed of our inadequate infrastructure. I remember a visit to Alaska where I stayed for a night in a small village. There were no sewers there, and so what? The Americans were not embarrassed. In any case, I believe that the remaining restrictions are Cold War remnants that will be removed as soon as possible.

Stanislav Kondrashov (*Izvestia*)

The Cold War began with the political and military postwar split of the world and is finishing before our eyes. It is ending because there is no longer a frenzied ideological irreconcilability implicit in East-West relations. We used to be leading a crusade against capitalism, invoking a slogan of the coming world revolution. And therein lie the roots of the Cold War--roots as dated as the revolutionary dogmas about world revolution and the final victory of socialism. We have not renounced these ideas in words but in actions. The cause of the changes lies in a sober look at our political relations both from the East and the West. The West does not perceive us as a fiend or as a source of aggression any more. The Cold War is no longer an extension of foreign policy.

The position of the West regarding the recent events in Europe can serve as an example. The West does not try to push the events forward. It behaves in such a way so as not to invoke anarchy and chaos. It does not intrude into the internal affairs of the Eastern European countries.

As for the nature of the events, they consist of a collapse of the "command-administrative system" of neo-Stalinist-Brezhnevite socialism. And we cannot but be happy about it. But because there is no other real model of socialism, the West has valid grounds for declaring the collapse of communism.

Our road to the present situation was filled with trials and mistakes. If the idea of world revolution became useless 10 years after 1917, the idea of world victory of socialism survived only to be "checked" in the Hungary of 1956 and the Czechoslovakia of 1968. During the same period, the West nurtured the idea of a crusade against socialism.

When we conceive of the Cold War as an ideological and military competition, we see that both East and West dropped the first component, whereas the second one is decreasing. Much depends on the level of manageability of the processes going on in the socialist countries now. Gorbachev approves of the course of events but worries about their tempo and possible turns. Here, a lot depends upon the people who are responsible for the fates of their nations, as well as the mood and spontaneity of the peoples.

A great deal depends upon the press. The end of the Cold War gives us a chance to write freely about world events. It is now possible to analyze once-forbidden topics. I have witnessed an evolution in the 30 years I have worked for the press. I never used Cold War clichés, nicknames, and so forth; I never compared Reagan with Hitler, as did some of my colleagues. I always stood for the commonsense ground. Now, sadly, when new vistas are open, we, the journalists, invent new rhetoric and banalities. Oftentimes we are not serious, focused, and analytical enough when writing about the world. Let us hope the next generation of reporters will use their opportunities more effectively.

Vitaly A. Korotich (*Ogonyok*)

The Cold War has always been here and it will exist in the future. I remember how at the most recent Supreme Soviet session a smiling general ran up to me and announced the U.S. landing in Panama, describing its feeble justification for the invasion. That was a happy day for our generals because on this pretext they could occupy half the world! For our military-industrial complex, the invasion of Panama was a gift, as Afghanistan was for the American military. I remember that on the eve of President Reagan's visit to Moscow an American battleship appeared off the Crimean coast. It was being pushed back, but the battleship came just under the batteries of our Black Sea fleet as if it were pleading: "Sink me, boys!" That was a hand of friendship from U.S. military leaders extended toward Soviet generals.

The same thing occurred with the Korean jumbo jet. That is why, in the climate of today's euphoria, we should not forget about the existence of a huge infrastructure of people who are not interested in our governments talking with each other. This huge group—in both the United States and the USSR—would die of hunger in conditions of normal bilateral relations. When relations are bad, it provides justification for the generals to get good money and privileges. A number of scholars can do nothing but "dethrone the imperialists." We must be realists; that is, we must understand that some components of the Cold War will remain, although it should never again become a dominant feature of politics. Pamyat and the John Birch Society have every right to exist in democratic society, but I would feel afraid if such constituencies started to rule the country. Both in the United States and in the Soviet Union there will be people who hate the Soviets or the Americans. That is always normal, but those people must not acquire too much power.

To sum it up, the Cold War as a social phenomenon of different countries will remain, though it will steadily fade away. The West has never before supported us so vigorously. The people of the West are well-off, and they are afraid to suffer from a possible fall of the silly elephant. All nations are ready to give us something in order to let us live as everybody else does. I became certain of this after recent talks with Henry Kissinger, Richard von Weizacker, Willy Brandt, and Helmut Schmidt. The world is ready to finance our return to civilized society. The phasing out of the Cold War goes hand in hand with the dying of totalitarianism in the East. We have seen that after the lid of totalitarianism was removed, many different things started to come out of it. Parliamentarian traditions, for example, have emerged in the Hungarian, Czechoslovak, and East German societies.

In my country, we also have diversity. You cannot write in a common impulse of Estonia and Turkmenia. Decentralization is task number one in the USSR. I feel sympathy for the Lithuanian experience. It has shown that in this country a communist party can win and keep the confidence of the people. On the other hand, events in Azerbaijan call for suppressive measures. One cannot put the border of equality between Vilnius and, say, Baku. The much-needed decentralization is a facet of freedom, and freedom leaves no place for totalitarianism.

We often take credit for having freed Eastern Europe from the Nazis, and we did. But we could not give them true liberty, because we ourselves were not free. Now those nations are achieving freedom on their own.

I fear that while the totalitarian lid is being lifted in the USSR our "innermost, represented qualities"—disconnection, hate, and spite—will surface. It will be more difficult for us than for the East Europeans to live like humans. But I am an optimist and therefore believe that the process of our society's integration into humanity, although painful, is natural.

A theory of external enemies is ideal for a totalitarian society. It forms a national swagger as well as an image of a bully who does not let us live well. The absence of sausage can be explained more easily by the existence of enemy intrigues than by deficiencies in our system. With the guidance of our administration, we look for the enemy somewhere else—we are called to beat the "kikes," intellectuals, and cosmopolitans: "Here comes the American who set the fire and destroyed whatever he possibly could." The Americans learned from us and propagandized the image of the villainous Russian communist.

Jingoism leads to cold wars. As soon as a person is rid of this hysteria he or she becomes a human being. Chauvinists and witch hunters will never disapppear, but it is important not to let them run rampant.

As for our magazine, *Ogonyok,* certain restrictions do remain. But they concern only topics about our "friends." We could not write the truth about Ceausescu before his fall, for example. We had other bitter experiences as well. In his reminiscences, published by our magazine. Sergei Khrushchev wrote that Zhivkov had known about the expected removal of Nikita Khrushchev, Sergei's father. Immediately afterwards, Zhivkov phoned Gorbachev, and I had to write an explanation. After *Ogonyok* referred to "a short period of stagnation" in the German Democratic Republic, Honnecker sent a note of protest, and we had to make apologies. Since then we have decided to be somewhat more cautious.

In any case, such unpleasantries constitute a temporary phenomenon destined into oblivion along with the other aspects of the Cold War epoch.

Vsevolod Ovchinnikov (*Pravda*)

The answer to the question of whether the Cold War is over depends not only on the warming up of international relations or the weakening of "hard" rhetoric of the press relaying the words of statesmen. The end of the Cold War depends mostly on the military situation, and that is what an international affairs reporter must take into account.

Let us analyze the international situation. On the one hand, we see a warming of international relations. On the other, the process of arms reduction has not taken such a good direction. What do I mean here? U.S.-Soviet military opposition stemmed from the American challenge of a nuclear monopoly. We became engaged in a nuclear buildup on the surface, mainly, and these surface forces are being reduced now. There are practically no small- and medium-range missiles left in Europe. The tempo of conventional force reduction is rather high. We have even agreed to an asymmetry in this realm. At the same time, there is no reply to Mikhail Gorbachev's proposals made in Krasnoyarsk and Vladivostok (regarding reduction of naval forces). Because of the U.S. military potential in the Pacific and other situations, potential activity in the skies rises. The seas become reserves of the Cold War. U.S. unwillingness to agree to some reduction there does not permit me to say that a Cold War resumption is no longer possible. We should always remember that the next step in arms control—a 50 percent cut in strategic nuclear missiles—with the United States objecting to inclusion of the navy and the air force, will aggravate the situation. The United States argues that both the navy and the air force are important for a naval power like America that depends greatly on imports. This may be true, but this stand imposes on us the most expensive arms race of all—that in the air and on the seas. It would not make naval routes any safer. The military advantages of the states would not guarantee stability in the world. A journalist must take all this into account when considering the question, "Is the Cold War over?" I am not a conservative, but when asked serious questions regarding the fate of the world, I prefer analysis to euphoria.

The enemy image—the USSR's image as a potential aggressor—is diluted now, and few people believe in it. But if the strategic imbalance remains on its present course, it would be impossible to say the Cold War is over.

Regarding the work of journalists, there are no restrictions left. The officials became accessible. I have not been getting any direction for the last five years. I can interact freely with the people from the Central Committee or the Foreign Ministry. They express their views; I can agree or not. With the possible establishment of a multiparty system in this country Soviet journalism should become a mosaic of different opinions and approaches (including to the Cold War issues).

Vladimir Pozner (anchor, Soviet television)

The Cold War is over in the strictest sense of military confrontation between the two superpowers and their allies. To begin with, the Eastern bloc is no longer a bloc. The Soviet Union itself is changing very rapidly, and I would not be surprised if, say in five years, it is a different country, a different kind of federation; it may not even consist of 15 republics. Such speculation in itself makes the Cold War something in the past.

However, I don't think it's right to say that the spirit of rivalry has completely disappeared between East and West, and this relationship is reflected in the media. Here is a typical example—and, of course, by the time this appears in print, things may have changed very much: Consider the way the media in the West are treating the events in Lithuania. The phraseology is very much Cold War phraseology. There is not much of an effort made to explain anything at all to the viewer or reader. The reporting is all based on the notions that have been built up over the 45 years of the Cold War. When you get a headline saying "Free Lithuania!" it is very much in the context of what people in the West have always thought about the Soviet Union: that it is a country that has oppressed its own people, who are slaves of the system; hence "Free Lithuania!" There is no talk about the difficulty of breaking up the relationships that have existed for fifty years and that include complex economic, political, social, and other ties.

I bring up the Lithuanian example just to show that although the Cold War is over the mentality is still very much in place. It takes very little for individual people and for the media to revert to the Cold War postures of the recent past. I have compared it to someone who starts to stand from a seated position. I feel that we all are in this position: We've started to get up but we haven't completely straightened up yet we're no longer sitting down. It's much easier to go back to where we were and sit down again rather than to straighten up. That is very much what the Cold War mentality is about. There is a change—it is beginning in the mindset of both East and West, but it is this process of beginning to get up. As soon as anything happens to the East or West that is reminiscent of what we had before, we all tend to sit back in the old postures. You will continue to see in the media for a while the almost conditioned reflex of two or three generations of people who have grown up in Cold War circumstances.

Alexander Pumpyansky (*Novoye Vremya*)

Malta has issued a stamp: "The Cold War Is Over." I was at the summit and can testify to it. Malta signaled that the civilized West was ready to put an end to the Cold War.

The Cold War is a composition of two elements: a broken world and a split nucleus. In the prenuclear age, the broken world was tolerable, normal, or expected, depending on one's view of world progress. In the nuclear age, it turned into a nightmare. The world was made hopping mad, and the split nucleus threatened us with a blowup (as well as insured against it, a fact we preferred to ignore).

Since the 1962 Cuban missile crisis the threat of the split nucleus has become clear for everybody. The 1970s détente was born out of the common wish not to be blown up as a result of overzealousness in security matters (i.e., in stockpiling arms). A magic formula consisting of just four letters was discovered: SALT. Our leaders thought then, let us control the strategic arms little by little and everything will be all right. In all other areas, they thought, one could go on in the old way. One could build a giant radar scope in Krasmoyarsk in the naive hope that the Americans would not notice it. One could take from the Helsinki Accords what was beneficial—inviolability of the borders—and ignore the other side of the issue—human rights. One could ignore the opinion of a hundred nations—the whole world community, including one's own people—and lead a "limited" war in a neighboring country for years. If the brass, the ideologists, or the politicians wanted something they could go ahead. The Cold War would ride out the indulgence.

That was a two-way street. The Cold War was a giant and successful joint venture with a turnover of billions of rubles and dollars and full employment. What it produced was another matter: an arms race, hatred, and the schizophrenia of mutual hysteria.

"The enemy is at the doorsteps!" There was some logic in this outcry. When the enemy was at the door, one had to tighten the belt and shut up. Then the thinking person became a dissident, an alien agent, an enemy of the people, and human rights became "so-called human rights" that were an "ideological subversion." As to our poverty, we could either take no notice of it or be proud of it as an ideologically purer entity than foreign or alien well-being. When at the confrontation line, the trenches are dug. In the rear, the Potemkin villages are built. And it is hard to say which is the original and which is secondary.

Thank God for the new thinking of which the results quickly became evident: Reagan at Red Square, Gorbachev with Reagan and Bush with the Statue of Liberty in the background. These glimpses symbolized the fading away of the Cold War. The revolutionary tornado in Eastern Europe showed that the new thinking was not just words but also deeds. The giant Potemkin village, the wall of the socialist camp created in accordance with Stalin's design, has collapsed. Since our perestroika, socialism in Europe has obtained a human face. The words about our common European house, the joint civilization to which both the East and West belong, have obtained a deep meaning. The break of the world is being overcome. There remain no fundamental reasons for the Cold War.

What lies ahead? Something wonderful. The year 1990 is to become a year of real disarmament. Political barriers in economic and other areas of cooperation with the West are to be removed. Is this enough? I am afraid not. The West will come to meet us, but are we ready for the meeting? The West will come to trade, but what products of ours can we trade? Because the idea not to betray our principles in economy means more than to make the economy modern, competent, and open, the present no-go situation will remain indefinitely.

After the Cold War comes the "Cold Peace" or, more accurately, a lukewarm peace. That is a major step forward, but the step is a short one. The step is guaranteed, from our side, by the revolution in consciousness, though not a total one. Alas, judging by the debates in higher spheres, I cannot but take into account different attempts of counterrevolution in consciousness, although I continue to hope for the better. I hope that from the field of consciousness the revolution will intrude into the political and socioeconomic spheres. Only then will the Cold War pass into oblivion and the real peace come.

Yuri Romantsov (TASS)

The Cold War in the mass media is a derivative of the Cold War in politics. It develops depending on the political situation. Nowadays, the Cold War in politics is subsiding, a situation immediately reflected in the state of the mass media. Despite the desire to say so, it is still too early to proclaim the final stage of the Cold War. Old times pull us back. The way of thinking that both military men and journalists shaped during Cold War times presses upon us. Not everybody is eager to get rid of the Cold War stereotypes. I mean not only Soviet but also American journalists.

The Cold War started with the famous Fulton speech by Winston Churchill. In my opinion the speech underscored the policy that had been conducted by both East and West. To blame the West as the only initiator of the Cold War is a mistake. Since the 1920s the same enemy image was being created by the USSR, and a substantial part of the USSR was involved in the creation of the postwar situation that we call the Cold War. I could never be persuaded that all European countries liberated by the West voluntarily went the Western way of civilization, while those liberated by the Red Army had chosen our way of development. Neither side played a totally clean game.

I am not completely sure we will not return to a Cold War atmosphere. The situation in Eastern Europe is not stable. I see it as being less possible that the Cold War's return will be from the West, whereas from the East it is still not unlikely. If perestroika continues, we can expect the end of confrontation. If that process is stopped, expect bad times.

Professional solidarity exists among Soviet and American journalists. This also works against the Cold War. And that existed even during the worst period of confronation, as I saw during my 10-year stay in the United States. TASS has close and proper relations with the Associated Press and United Press International. TASS's computer is located in and even served by the AP office in New York City. That proves complete mutual confidence.

American journalism attracts me in every sense except its excessive orientation toward sensational events. What attracts me most is its efficiency and trust in reporters. In the United States news is rarely corrected by the editors. We are trying now to use this model. I also like the way the U.S. reporters stand above the facts, render them impartially, and do not associate their own or the governmental point of view with the goings-on. We should learn from this objective approach. Politicization is a hindrance in the work of Soviet agency reporters. We try to fight the politicization, but with little success because from their earliest schooling Soviet people are educated in a different way. News should bear no ideological taint. I envy American journalists also because they have a large market to which they sell their product. Unlike the USSR, the United States has real newspapers. I cannot call *Pravda* or *Izvestia* newspapers, as a result of their small amounts of space usually covered with huge items that are practically indigestible.

If these conditions for the healthy functioning of journalism are created, what is contrary now to common sense—the enemy-image propaganda and Cold War ideology—will fall into oblivion.

Nikolai Setunsky (*Echo of the Planet*)

A diplomatic dictionary issued in the USSR in 1988 considers *Cold War* to be a term used only in regard to the policies of the United States and other imperialist countries against the USSR during the postwar period. I think this definition has some flaws because any war is a condition existing between two or more countries. Here we have a contribution to the Cold War situation from only one side—the United States. It is strongly ideologically motivated. In my opinion the Cold War is a global or regional policy of military, political, and economic confrontation between the two groups of states.

With the new thinking becoming stronger, we may say that some of the Cold War factors do not exist any more or that they have become extremely weak. At the same time some of the factors and features remain—the situation in the arms control sphere, for example. We have a strategic and nuclear arms reduction on the one hand, and the continuation of the arms race on the other. That is why it is still early to speak about the end of the Cold War in at least some of its aspects. There still exists a network of military bases around the USSR. Military blocs still remain. In these areas we can only talk about prospects in removing the Cold War factors. But taking into consideration the new thinking concept, the West's principal decision to stop the arms race, the pace of arms control talks, and the agreement not to use force in international relations, we see the absence of many important elements of the Cold War. In principle there is no future for the Cold War.

Speaking about the Cold War now I would use these words: "came to its end," "became bankrupt," or "declined." But I would not say that it is over. The atmosphere of confidence is too fragile between East and West. Nobody knows what will happen if there is something done against Cuba, or if the two Germanies reunite and the former German Democratic Republic joins NATO. I see no guarantees against a possible change by this or any other U.S. administration on the question of arms control. One cannot deny the possibility of such developments. Although it is only a hypothesis, the possibility of a setback and return to the Cold War atmosphere remains real.

It is too early to say the Cold War is over. Renaissance is possible. Considering the interrelations between the Cold War and the mass media, I see two aspects. First, the anticommunism of the Western media was always considered a manifestation of the Cold War, which is not quite true. Anti-communism existed in the Western media before World War II. Anti-imperialist, anticapitalist propaganda was conducted in the Soviet Union long before the Cold War. The Cold War only galvanized such propaganda. That is why, although we have two ecological poles, the opposition of ideas will remain, though this opposition will not necessarily be linked with the Cold War.

The enemy image is a manifestation of the propaganda war, a part of the Cold War. With the thaw in international relations this image will erode. At the same time the hostility of ideological, political, and economic structures will remain. I think the notion of "enemy" will be replaced by the notion of "opponent." But the new notion will function only at the individual, not at the state-to-state, level.

Yuri Zhukov (*Pravda*)

The Cold War started in October 1917. It was initiated by capitalist countries. I remember those times very well. As a boy I witnessed U.S. intervention at our far eastern borders. We stood up to it, but, unfortunately, this lesson did not teach the imperialists. The confrontation took the shape of an economic fight. It was the West that treated us with intolerance. The bourgeoisie tried military means in 1941 for the second time.

In general, the problem of the Cold War is not a question of just a propaganda struggle. The essence of the problem lies in the way we build the relations between two systems: the capitalist system and the socialist one.

After World War II the West continued to count on its military might, which went together with the development of the propagandistic aspect of the Cold War. I remember the scandal with *Collier's* magazine. The magazine printed a fantasy story that rendered the "real" plan to start nuclear war against the USSR in 1957. The story also discussed the possibilities of using Russian émigrés and dissidents in the fight against the Soviet state. Another story printed then by *U.S. News and World Report* and called "Subversive Tactics in the Cold War" said that Washington planned "to organize military units headed by the Americans and kill leading Communists." As we see, the U.S. press was propagandizing both the Cold War and a hot war. Naturally, we must admit our own part of the responsibility for the creation of such a hysterical climate in society. The politics of Stalin were catastrophic. If after Potsdam the USSR had led a policy based on Lenin's idea of peaceful coexistence, much aggravation could have been avoided. Both sides pushed each other in the Cold War direction. Our mistakes in Iran, in 1945, and the Berlin blockade promoted the creation of NATO. French newspapers so frightened the people in 1947 that I remember seeing long lines waiting for visas at the Spanish embassy. All of the foregoing promoted the Cold War.

Khrushchev, himself a product of Stalinism, did much to bring to life Lenin's thoughts on peaceful coexistence. International tensions relaxed, a situation attributable to Khrushchev's trips to India and Burma in 1955, as well as his trips to the United States and France. I participated in the Soviet delegations during those trips. It was then that we realized what would become a reality only 30 years later. A Cold War maneuver, namely, the provocation of the U-2 spy plane sent deep into our territory by the United States, did its job. I am sure that incident was intentional, meant to drive

Khrushchev out of his wits, and the plan succeeded. One could calm the situation but not Khrushchev. At the 1960 Paris summit, just two weeks after the incident with the plane, Khrushchev demanded apologies from Eisenhower. I took part in the summit and remember the red-as-a-lobster face of Eisenhower. Khrushchev played the role of the furious and offended father of a family. The U.S. president refused to say he was sorry. Then Charles de Gaulle became agitated: He wanted to be a peacemaker there. This is an example of how Cold War psychology did not let us use a chance to come closer to each other.

It was also hard to become closer in the Brezhnev years. I think his foreign policy up to the 1975 Helsinki Accords was successful. That was a real zigzag toward the end of the Cold War, not a stagnation period. The well-known follies and mistakes began after 1975. The result was that after April 1985, we had to start everything afresh. Gorbachev returned to the source of Lenin and early Khrushchev, to Brezhnev before Helsinki.

The essence of the new thinking is directed toward the dismantling of confrontation. We must acknowledge that for the time being there remain two world systems. Some say we will return to the bosom of capitalism, but they are wrong. We shall not return to the capitalist system. What we are doing is stripping away revolutionary extremism. We want to realize the idea of peaceful coexistence with the West. And nothing more. It is also not true that Eastern Europe is returning to capitalism. One cannot believe "ostentatious unanimity." Look at the recent events in Romania. Our leaders believed the people were fond of Ceausescu, but in fact the people stormed the streets with the slogan, "Death to Ceausescu!"

Let us not oversimplify. I think that the Cold War remains, even in the field of propaganda. Just take a look at the statement by George Bush about the fall of communism, about the United States as the only superpower left. The Cold War remains. One can only speak about aggravation or relaxation of international tension. Based on the chauvinistic campaign in connection with the U.S. intervention in Panama, Cold War propaganda is very much alive in America.

As for the USSR, we have no supporters of the Cold War, either in the propagandistic or the political field.

Leonid Zolotarevsky (Gosteleradio)

The Cold War started in October 1917, the time of the socialist revolution in Russia. It has been always and everywhere a flip side of the hot war. These two were not always in step with each other—that might be the difference between them.

In the mass media, the Cold War approaches the two ideologies at the two sides of the Berlin Wall. It was important that the Wall not let them touch each other, because this was the only means of keeping the Cold War below the freezing point. Quarantine is vital for the preservation of ideologies. When the opposite ideologies start to make contact, the Cold War is coming to its end. I believe that the coming end of the Cold War is a result of the fall of the Berlin Wall, with the help of the modern media.

Interaction of opposite ideological systems is an objective process. These interactions become less acute and show that our age of modern mass media and high technology weapons for a hot war do not accept the Cold War psychology. The reason is that once you start using mass media "weapons," you can easily come to real weapons of mass extermination.

So, is the Cold War over? I think it cannot be over while there remain certain influential groups of the opposite ideologies' standard-bearers. They believe that there must not be any interactions and that only a state of conflict is permitted. Such groups exist both here and in the West, although their influence has waned in the past five or ten years. The groups consist of some military men, bureaucratic structures, and, last but not least, common people with conservative thinking. We have a long way to go on the road to overcoming the Cold War mentality, but I see the guarantees of our success in democracy and glasnost becoming stronger and stronger.

In our cooperation with the Western media the only difficulty left is the financial problem. Sponsors' interests dominate the media in the West. As for us, we are always reminded that the ruble is still not a convertible currency. And finally, we have one more problem in our convergent times: We still have different time zones. This "obstacle," however, cannot be removed.

Valentin Zorin (USA-Canada Institute)

There are broad and narrow meanings of the Cold War. Until recently the Cold War meant the propaganda war. In this narrow meaning, it has not stopped and is unlikely to stop soon. In the wider meaning, as the whole system of East-West relations, it began with the Hiroshima bombing. That bombing was aimed not at Japan; the intention was to bring the USSR to its knees. Therefore, I can only blame the United States as the initiator of the Cold War.

Neither do I want to depict the USSR as a virgin raped by the West. To say this would be to distort history. The Cold War suited Stalin. The original idea of the Marshall Plan meant some help for the USSR as well as other countries, but Stalin did not want it. What he wanted was confrontation. President

Truman was very much like him in that he could not be trusted. To my mind, Truman would not allow the positive ideas of the Marshall Plan to be realized. That was the beginning. The whole system of East-West relations, from August 1945 to the Malta summit, was founded on the Cold War principles.

That was a period of real war, not a postwar period; a war for extermination of the enemy. All means except open military clashes were used. Complete victory was at stake. Understanding of the no-win situation of nuclear war paved the way to rapprochement.

Is the Cold War over? I interviewed Mikhail Gorbachev for Soviet television at the end of the Malta summit and asked him that question. He answered: "It is ending." I asked, "Is ending or has ended?" He replied, "It came to its end, but we cannot but take into account the remaining structures and instruments of the Cold War."

It is much more difficult to put an end to the Cold War than to finish an ordinary war. It is a long process. Human psychology must be changed as well. Just look at the ecstasy of the American public during the intervention in Panama—wasn't this a Cold War way of thinking?

Malta was a watershed. The new U.S. administration had made its choice. To prove the West's readiness to end the Cold War, imagine what would have happened if the Berlin Wall had been destroyed three years earlier, during the Cold War years. In 1989 the West showed its responsibility and did not rejoice at the breakup of communism; that would have been shortsighted. What we are seeing is a breakup of a Stalinist model of socialism. Consider a possible breakup of the U.S. economy. Three trillion dollars is quite a debt, a time bomb for the national economy. If it exploded, columnists would be shortsighted to call it a breakup of capitalism. Crisis is a step in development and is a possibility everywhere. But crisis is not necessarily a breakup.

I believe the Cold War is coming to an end. Malta was a fork in the road on which political development traveled to the end of the Cold War. The end of the Cold War has a broad meaning, because the basis of the prior order has eroded. First, humankind realized it could not solve its problems by use of the military. Second, countries encountered global problems that would be best solved in a joint effort. There was an objective basis for both the beginning and the end of the Cold War.

In the mass media the Cold War has not stopped. It will go on. But this is politics, not a strategy. Political contradictions between the United States and the USSR will also remain. Because of them, time and again the propaganda methods of the Cold War will be used. I am afraid that journalism will be the last fortification of the Cold War, and I say this with sorrow.

Appendix: Turning Points in 45 Years of Cold War

1946 (March 5): Churchill's "Iron Curtain" speech in US.

1947 (March 12): Truman doctrine launched: US to oppose communism everywhere.

1948 (April 1): Soviet blockage of Berlin starts.

1949 (May 12): Blockage ends.

1949 (March 18): NATO established; Soviet Union retaliates by founding the Warsaw Pact.

1950 (June 25): Korean war.

1953 (March 5): Stalin dies.

1953 (June 17): Soviet Union crushes East German uprising.

1956 (October 26): Hungarian uprising crushed by Soviet tanks.

1959 (January 2): Cuban revolution.

1960 (May 5): Moscow shoots down American U2 spy plane.

1961 (April 19): Bay of Pigs.

1961 (August 31): Berlin Wall built.

1962 (October): Cuban missile crisis.

1964 (August 7): US marines land in Vietnam.

1968 (August 21): Soviet Union invades Czechoslovakia.

1969 (October 21): Willy Brandt launches Ostpolitik.

1972: SALT 1 missile agreement.

1975: Helsinki agreements on security and human rights.

1979 (December 27): USSR invades Afghanistan.

1985 (March 10): Gorbachev elected.

1989: Revolutions in Eastern Europe.

1989 (September 11): Berlin Wall begins to come down.

References Consulted

Periodicals

"After the Cold War," *Newsweek* cover story, May 15, 1989, pp. 20-25.

Stanley Hoffman, "What Should We Do In the World?" *Atlantic Monthly*, October 1989, pp. 84-96.

Charles Krauthammer, "Beyond the Cold War," *The New Republic*, December 19, 1988, p. 14-19

Kenneth Maxwell and Susan L. Clark, "Soviet Dilemmas in Latin America: Pragmatism or Ideology?" *Critical Issues*, Council on Foreign Relations, New York, 1989.

John Mueller, "Enough Rope: The Cold War Was Lost, Not Won," *The New Republic*, July 3, 1989, pp. 14-16.

John Newhouse, "The Diplomatic Round—Eternal Severities," *The New Yorker*, October 23, 1989, pp. 100-30.

Saul Pett, "The Cold War: Ended, Ending or Pausing—A Surreal Struggle Fed by Mutual Fear," *AP Newsfeatures Report*, August 7, 1989.

Radek Sikorski, "The Coming Crack-Up of Communism: Decline or Fall," *National Review*, January 27, 1989, pp. 28-46.

Rochelle L. Stanfield, "Beyond the Cold War," *National Journal*, September 16, 1989, pp. 225-258.

Gore Vidal, "Our Television Politburo: Cue the Green God, Ted," *The Nation*, August 7, 1989, pp. 1, 170-174.

Dennis Wrong, "The Waning of the Cold War," *Dissent*, 1989, pp. 192-197.

Books

Graham T. Allison & William L. Ury, eds., *Windows of Opportunity: From Cold War to Peaceful Competition in U.S.-Soviet Relations* (Cambridge: Ballinger, 1989).

Serwyn Bialer, *The Soviet Paradox: External Expansion, Internal Decline* (New York: Knopf, 1986).

Zbigniew Brzezinski, *The Grand Failure: The Birth and Death of Communism in the Twentieth Century* (New York: Scribners, 1989).

David P. Calleo, *Beyond American Hegemony: The Future of the Western Alliance* (New York: Basic Books, 1987).

Stephen F. Cohen, *Rethinking the Soviet Experience: Politics and History Since 1917* (New York: Oxford, 1985).

Raymond L. Garthoff, *Detente and Confrontation: American-Soviet Relations From Nixon to Reagan* (Washington: Brookings, 1985).

Marshall Goldman, *Gorbachev's Challenge: Economic Reform in the Age of High Technology* (New York: Norton, 1987).

Moshe Lewin, *The Gorbachev Phenomenon: A Historical Interpretation* (Berkeley: University of California Press, 1988).

Richard M. Nixon, *1999: Victory Without War* (New York: Simon & Schuster, 1988).

William Pfaff, *Barbarian Sentiments: How the American Century Ends* (New York: Hill & Wang, 1988).

Index

About the Editors and Contributors

Elena Androunas is a Senior Research Fellow with the Faculty of Journalism at Moscow State University. Her primary areas of study include the economics of mass media industries, media monopolies, and new information technologies. Earlier, Androunas served as a visiting scholar at the Annenberg School of Communications at the University of Pennsylvania. Professionally, she has worked as a staffer for a local radio station and as a stringer for a regional newspaper. Author of over 40 scholarly articles, she has coauthored three volumes on Western media and is author of *Business and Propaganda* and the forthcoming *Information Elite*. Androunas holds an M.A. in journalism and a Ph.D. in history from Moscow State University.

Won Ho Chang is a professor at the School of Journalism of the University of Missouri. He received his Ph.D. in mass communication from the University of Iowa in 1972. He is the director of the journalism computer center and of the International Graduate Journalism program at Missouri.

Everette E. Dennis is Executive Director of the Gannett Center for Media Studies. Formerly he was Dean of the School of Journalism at the University of Oregon and Professor of Journalism and Director of Graduate Studies at the University of Minnesota. He has also taught at Kansas State, where he was acting head of the journalism department. A past president of the Association for Education in Journalism and Mass Communication, Dennis is author or editor of 15 books and many articles, including *Reshaping the Media, The Cost of Libel, The Media Society,* and *Understanding Mass Communication.* He has held fellowhips at the Harvard Law School, Nieman Foundation, and John F. Kennedy School of Government, all at Harvard University.

Donna Eberwine was until recently the Executive Editor of *Deadline,* the bimonthly research bulletin of the Center for War, Peace, and the News Media. Previously she was a senior editor at *Nuclear Times* magazine and a freelance radio and print reporter in Central America for the Latin American News Service and for newspapers including *The San Diego Union,* the *Minneapolis Star and Tribune,* and *The Miami Herald.* She is currently an editor for the Inter-American Development Bank.

Larissa Fedotova is a Senior Research Fellow at the Faculty of Journalism of the Moscow University. She received her M.A. in journalism from the Faculty of Journalism of the Moscow University in 1966 and her Ph.D. in 1969. Her research activities cover public opinion and content analysis of the media.

George Gerbner is Professor of Communications and Dean Emeritus of the Annenberg School of Communications at the University of Pennsylvania. Before joining the University in 1964 he taught at the University of Illinois and the University of Southern California. Gerbner also has served on the staff of the *San Francisco Chronicle*. He has directed U.S. and multinational mass communications projects under the auspices of the National Science Foundation, UNESCO, and the U.S. Office of Education. He is executive editor of the quarterly *Journal of Communication* and is author and editor of numerous articles on mass communication research.

Daniel C. Hallin is Associate Professor of Communication at the University of California, San Diego. His research on the Reagan/Gorbachev summits was done in collaboration with Paolo Mancini of the Universita degli Studi di Perugia. Further discussions of this research can be found in the journal *Communication* and in Jay G. Blumler, Jack M. McLeod, and Karl Erik Rosengren, *Communication and Culture Across Space and Time: Prospects of Comparative Analysis.*

Svetlana G. Kolesnik is a Research Fellow with the Faculty of Journalism at Moscow State University. Her areas of research include the history of television and television journalism. Author of a number of scholarly works, she holds an M.A. in journalism and a Ph.D. in history from Moscow State University.

Liu Liqun is a Senior Research Fellow of the Institute of Journalism of the Academy of Social Sciences of the Chinese People's Republic. He studied in the United States and is conducting research on U.S. and other Western media.

Marius Aleksas Lukosiunas is a postgraduate student with the Faculty of Journalism at Moscow State University. He is currently studying journalism theory and objectivity as viewed by American media theorists. Earlier, from 1984 to 1987, Lukosiunas worked as an anchor for Lithuanian television. He received his M.A. in journalism from Vilnius University.

Robert Karl Manoff is the director of the Center for War, Peace, and the News Media and research professor in the Department of Journalism and Mass Communication at New York University. He has been the managing editor of *Harper's* magazine and the editor of the *Columbia Journalism Review* and has written widely on press issues, nuclear issues, and Soviet affairs in such publications as the *Bulletin of Atomic Scientists,* the *Journal of Communication, The Quill,* and *Harper's.* He is the coeditor of *Reading the News* and *The Image of Politics and the Politics of Image: The Media and the Political Process.*

Ellen Mickiewicz, Alben W. Barkley Professor of Political Science at Emory University, graduated from Wellesley College and received her Ph.D. from Yale University. Her most recent book, *Split Signals: Television and Politics in the Soviet Union,* was awarded the Electronic Media Book of the Year by the National Association of Broadcasters and the Broadcast Education Association. She is the author or editor of several books on Soviet studies; in addition, her articles have appeared in such journals as *Public Opinion Quarterly, Slavic Review,* and *Journal of Communication,* and in newspapers such as *The New York Times* and *Corriere della Sera.* She is Director of the Soviet Media and International Communications Program of The Carter Center of Emory University and is a Fellow in Soviet-American relations there.

Andrei G. Richter is a postgraduate student with the Faculty of Journalism at Moscow State University. He currently conducts research on the American media and industrial relations as reflected in the British press. Formerly, Richter served as an English teacher and also worked as an interpreter in Nigeria. He holds an M.A. in English from Kharkov University.

R. Michael Schiffer is an analyst at the Center for War, Peace, and the News Media. Previously he served on congressional staff and as an aide to the senior foreign policy advisor on the Dukakis presidential compaign. His writings on international security issues have appeared in the Center for International Relations' *Journal of International Affairs* as well as in publications of the Center for War, Peace, and the News Media.

Xu Yoakui is Deputy Director of the Institute of Journalism of the Academy of Social Sciences of the Chinese People's Republic in Beijing. He is an expert in Chinese and Soviet media.

Yassen N. Zassoursky is Dean of the Faculty and a Professor of Journalism at Moscow State University. He previously served as Editor of the Publishing House of Foreign Literature. He has lectured at the University of Michigan, the University of Minnesota, Stanford University, and the Annenberg School of Communications and also has worked as a correspondent for *Literaturnaya Gazeta*. He is the editor or author of several works, including *Modern Bourgeois Theories of Journalism* and *Twentieth Century American Literature*. He also edited the Russian translation of H. I. Schiller's *The Mind Managers* and *Communications and Cultural Domination*. Zassoursky received his M.A. in English from the Institute of Foreign Languages in Moscow and his Ph.D. in American literature from Moscow University.